To my darling daughter, Esmé, who makes me laugh every day
G.J.

For Grandma and Grandpa Taylor
J.T.

First published 2022 by Walker Books Ltd
87 Vauxhall Walk, London SE11 5HJ

2 4 6 8 10 9 7 5 3 1

This book has been typeset in Avenir and AbneyandTeal

Printed in China

British Library Cataloguing in Publication Data: a catalogue
record for this book is available from the British Library

ISBN 978-1-4063-9567-9

www.walker.co.uk

WALKER BOOKS
AND SUBSIDIARIES
LONDON • BOSTON • SYDNEY • AUCKLAND

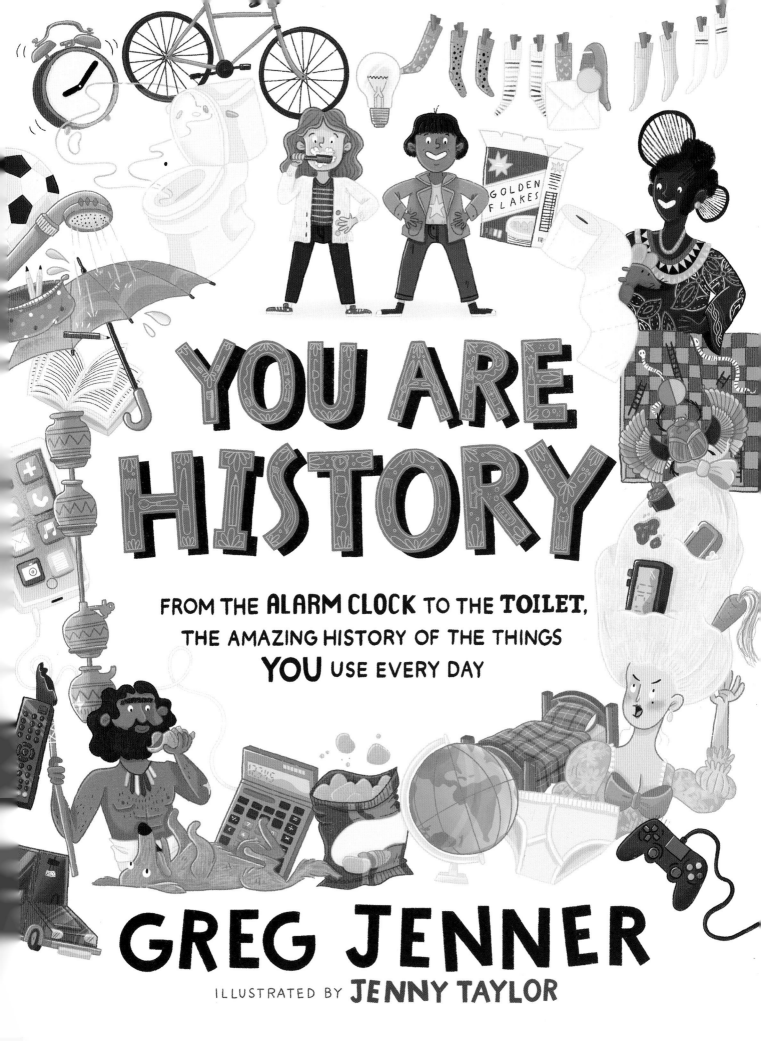

YOU ARE HISTORY

FROM THE **ALARM CLOCK** TO THE **TOILET**, THE AMAZING HISTORY OF THE THINGS **YOU** USE EVERY DAY

GREG JENNER

ILLUSTRATED BY **JENNY TAYLOR**

CONTENTS

INTRODUCTION

Hi! How are you – very well, I hope? Thanks for picking up this book. I'm guessing you were lured in by the fun front cover, drawn by my fantastic illustrator Jenny, but now you're checking to see if the words on the inside are really boring, right…? Wise decision, I salute your suspicious instincts. By all means have a little peek inside and decide if you like what you see. I'll just wait here until you return…

DUM DI DUM…

Oh, you're back? And it wasn't too dull? Phew! All right, let me introduce myself properly, then.

Hello, I'm Greg, and I'm a "Public Historian". That means I don't just study the past, I also try to make history super enjoyable for other people. I do that by writing books, hosting podcasts, helping out on films and video games, and by working on funny things (like CBBC's "Horrible Histories"). Many of my fellow historian pals are super brainy and super serious, but I'm a big fan of being a little bit silly. In fairness, I can't help it – I am a very silly man – but it's also because I think laughing is a great way to learn stuff. It's what helped me fall in love with history when I was young.

Unlike most historians, I don't specialise in only one bit of history. I don't just do the Romans, or the Vikings, or the Aztecs… No, I like ALL OF IT, across the whole world, from the Stone Age right up to our modern Phone Age! And I'm really, really interested in the ordinary stuff: toilets, food, underpants, etc.!

Obviously, history is full of incredible stories about bejewelled kings and queens, mega-famous historical celebrities, fascinating inventors, important thinkers, yada yada yada … and, yes, they're definitely brilliant fun to hear about. But I'm also interested in what daily life was like for people like you and me. How could things have been different if we'd been born ages ago, in a different part of the world?

So, in this book, I want to do two things:

1) I want to give you a few giggles (I will also accept snorts, titters, chuckles, ROFLs, hoots, honks and laughs).

2) I want to guide you through your ordinary day, and reveal how all that normal, boring stuff actually has an AMAZING history going back hundreds, or even thousands, of years. We'll start with the alarm clock that gets you out of bed in the morning, and we'll bounce through getting washed and dressed, travelling to school, the stuff you use in your classroom, the gadgets you enjoy when you're home, the food and drinks you'll devour, the pets you might play with, the activities you'll enjoy, and we'll end up back in your nice, cosy bed.

You may feel very modern, but every day you're doing the same things that our ancient ancestors did. You're just lucky to have cooler shoes and better Wi-Fi. Basically, YOU are history! So, let's get cracking on our journey, which means thumping the OFF switch on your noisy alarm clock…

HOW TO WRITE BOOKS!

HISTORY 101

ALARM CLOCK

WAKEY WAKEY! It's time to get up, or else you'll be late for school. But how do you know when it's time to get up? Maybe you're like me: a snoring sleepyhead who has to be dragged from their lovely, warm duvet every morning. You probably use a clever gadget to startle you from your dreams – an alarm clock. Electronic alarm clocks are powered by tiny quartz crystals that vibrate a whopping 32,768 times per second! This technology was first used in gadgets you could buy in the 1970s, so surely alarm clocks can't be that old, can they? Well, prepare to be AMAZED!

PLATO'S WATER CLOCK

One of the first alarm clocks dates back an incredible 2,400 years, and was apparently made by ancient Greek philosopher Plato. He ran a famous school in Athens, but his students were like me – always oversleeping! So, the beardy brainbox built a wake-up system based on a water clock (the Greek word was *clepsydra*). These gadgets were already 1,000 years old by Plato's lifetime, and they measured time by letting water drain from one tank into another.

So, how did Plato's clock work? Annoyingly, we don't know! Plato left us loads of his big ideas about politics and how to be a good person, but not his clock instructions. Perhaps it whistled like a steam train, by forcing air out of a pipe? Or maybe it released brass balls that clanged noisily onto metal, a bit like when all the saucepans clatter out of my kitchen cupboard and bounce off my head! Who knows?

Either way, the smart thing about water clocks is that you can adjust them by pouring in more/less water, or making the holes in the pots bigger/smaller so the water trickles through faster/slower. So, maybe Plato's clock had a snooze option to allow for an extra long lie-in? I hope so!

SMELLING THE TIME

Not all clocks show the time. One thousand years ago, in medieval China, a *fire-clock* let you smell the time! Basically, it was an incense burner filled with exact measurements of incense that burned for one hour. When that hour passed, a metal ball dropped and made a loud chime sound. But the most brilliant part was anyone could walk into the room and sniff the air to know what time it was, because each hour had its own distinctive smell. Of course, it only works if you haven't got an even smellier teenage brother ponging up the place.

It smells like two o'clock!

KNOCKER-UPPERS

My favourite alarm clock from history was the beautifully named knocker-upper. And it wasn't even a gadget. No, it was a person!

In Queen Victoria's era (she reigned 1837–1901), a knocker-upper was someone who went up and down the streets of British towns with a long stick. Sure, they probably looked like pole-vaulters practising for the Olympics, but actually their job was to wake up all the factory workers by banging on windows with their pole. Funnily enough, sometimes the knocker-upper also needed waking up in time to do this job. And who woke up a knocker-upper? Well, a knocker-upper's knocker-upper, obviously! But I wonder who woke up the knocker-upper's knocker-upper … hmmm?

Ow! My face!

Shut your windows, then!

2 TOILET

I don't want to get too personal – after all, we've only just met! But, is it just me, or do you sometimes wake up in the morning and think, "Uh oh, I need to go to the loo!" In my country (the UK!) toilets tend to be indoors, in a room with a nearby sink for hygienic handwashing. You might assume that pretty much everyone gets to enjoy this modern luxury, but sadly there are four billion people in the world today who don't have safe access to toilet facilities. We're lucky to be able to pee in peace and safety. But our toilets haven't always been this way.

TAKE A SEAT

When you sit on a toilet seat, you're doing something very ancient. Yes, amazingly, our loo seat dates back to the period known as the Bronze Age, over 4,000 years ago. They were used in both ancient Egypt and the ancient Indus civilisation (which was based in what is now Pakistan and India). Seats could be carved from stone, built from bricks or made from simple wooden planks. People did their business into a chamber pot below the seat, or down a hole into a cesspit. The Indus were particularly advanced in their hygienic engineering: some of their houses were connected to drainage channels that carried waste away, so the person doing the pooing could flush away the smelly stuff with a bucket of water. Pretty impressive!

Toodle-oo, poo!

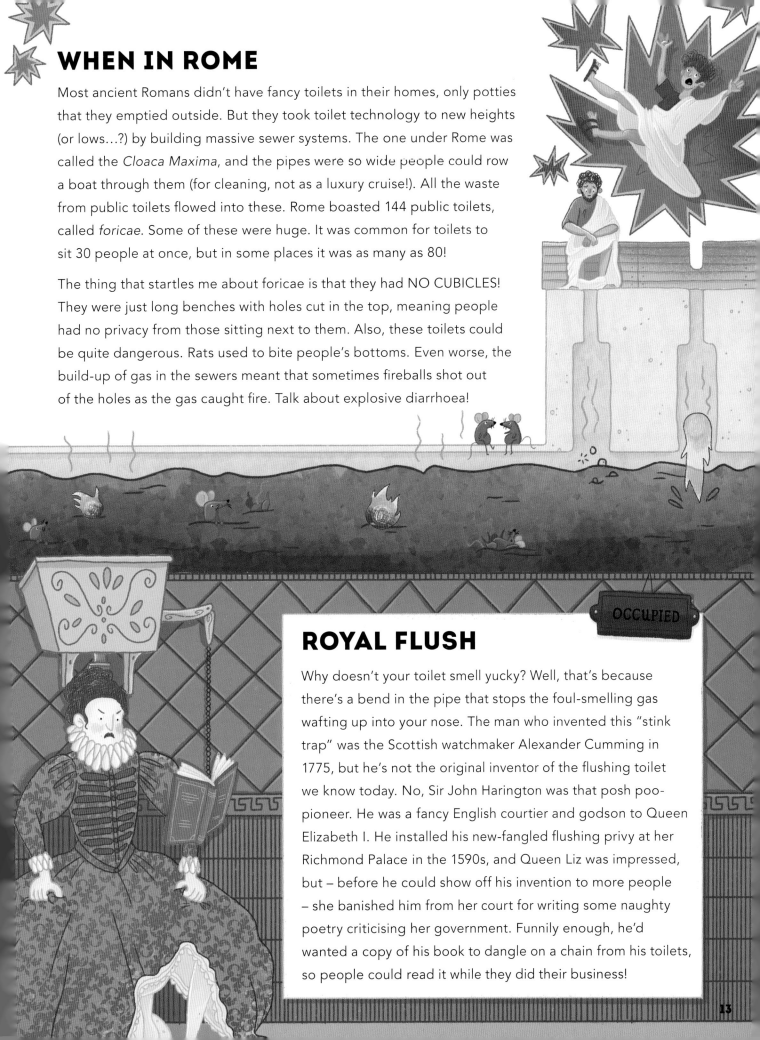

WHEN IN ROME

Most ancient Romans didn't have fancy toilets in their homes, only potties that they emptied outside. But they took toilet technology to new heights (or lows…?) by building massive sewer systems. The one under Rome was called the *Cloaca Maxima*, and the pipes were so wide people could row a boat through them (for cleaning, not as a luxury cruise!). All the waste from public toilets flowed into these. Rome boasted 144 public toilets, called *foricae*. Some of these were huge. It was common for toilets to sit 30 people at once, but in some places it was as many as 80!

The thing that startles me about foricae is that they had NO CUBICLES! They were just long benches with holes cut in the top, meaning people had no privacy from those sitting next to them. Also, these toilets could be quite dangerous. Rats used to bite people's bottoms. Even worse, the build-up of gas in the sewers meant that sometimes fireballs shot out of the holes as the gas caught fire. Talk about explosive diarrhoea!

OCCUPIED

ROYAL FLUSH

Why doesn't your toilet smell yucky? Well, that's because there's a bend in the pipe that stops the foul-smelling gas wafting up into your nose. The man who invented this "stink trap" was the Scottish watchmaker Alexander Cumming in 1775, but he's not the original inventor of the flushing toilet we know today. No, Sir John Harington was that posh poo-pioneer. He was a fancy English courtier and godson to Queen Elizabeth I. He installed his new-fangled flushing privy at her Richmond Palace in the 1590s, and Queen Liz was impressed, but – before he could show off his invention to more people – she banished him from her court for writing some naughty poetry criticising her government. Funnily enough, he'd wanted a copy of his book to dangle on a chain from his toilets, so people could read it while they did their business!

DON'T FALL IN!

Six hundred years ago, in medieval England, the person who emptied the toilet cesspit was called a *gongfermor*, and the stench of these pits was so bad that sometimes gongfermors would faint and drown in all the poo! One particularly unfortunate gongfermor was Richard the Raker. He cleaned other people's toilets in the 1300s, until one day he sat on his OWN toilet and it collapsed under his weight. He fell into his own poo and died. Oh no, poor guy!

This job stinks!

DON'T GET STUCK!

So, that was the worst-case scenario for toilet accidents. I guess the medium-case scenario was falling into the hole bum-first and getting embarrassingly stuck. This happened quite often at William Michie's Tavern in Virginia, USA, during the 1780s.

People visited the tavern before going to see President Thomas Jefferson's nearby house, but the holes in the toilet seat were a little *too* big, so people kept falling in. Michie was so annoyed at having to keep rescuing them, he hung a rope from the ceiling so people could pull themselves out!

You're meant to sit ON the toilet, not IN it!

TOILET PAPER  3

Of course, using the toilet requires cleaning ourselves afterwards, and these days the most common thing you'll find next to the toilet is perforated loo roll, probably made from recycled paper. As well as being a fun fancy dress option (you can wrap yourself up like an ancient Egyptian mummy), toilet paper is both very old and also not very old at all, depending on where in the world you look.

ON A ROLL

It was the ancient Chinese who first made paper, nearly 2,200 years ago, and they were using it for bottom-wiping by 1,500 years ago. But it was quite pricey and only affordable to the richest. Also, it didn't look like our modern loo roll. During the 1300s, the emperor's toilet paper was small, like ours today, but his courtiers had to use sheets as big as a hand towel! Presumably they had normal-sized bottoms, so maybe they tore strips off instead of using the whole thing?

Modern toilet paper was only introduced in North America in the 1850s, having been invented by a man named Joseph Gayetty. The tearable perforations between each piece arrived in the 1890s. What's more, until 1935, toilet paper sometimes had splinters in it. OUCH! Personally, I think splinter-free loo roll should be the bare minimum for my bare behind!

SHAREABLE SPONGES

As well as paper, lots of other things have been used to wipe people's bums. In ancient Rome, the public toilets (foricae) provided sponges on the end of a stick, which people dipped in salt water or vinegar, then used to wipe themselves. But the thing that makes me feel queasy is that they then handed this dirty sponge on a stick (called a xylospongium) to the stranger next to them! Can you imagine sharing someone else's used loo roll?! Urgh, no thanks…

Your turn!

READ IT AND WIPE

In the USA, corn is the most widely grown food, with a rich farming history going back thousands of years. But it wasn't just good for going into the body, it was also useful when things were on the way out! Yes, back in the early colonial days of America, 400 years ago, farmers would shuck off all the tasty sweetcorn, and be left with a long, soft cob that was perfect for wiping their rear ends.

However, by the 1700s, when newspapers started to be widely printed in Europe and North America, lots of people instead used torn-out pages of newspapers and magazines. Presumably the ink sometimes rubbed off on them, meaning maybe you could still read the articles on their bums. Or should we call it reading to the "bottom" of the page?!

In fact, by the 1800s, one of America's most famous magazines, the *Farmer's Almanac*, was even printed with a special hole in the pages so people could hang it up next to the toilet, ready to rip a page out. People complained when lots of magazines switched to printing on glossy paper in the 1930s, because it didn't feel so nice on their tushies!

STICKS AND STONES

Wiping materials weren't always super soft in the past. Indigenous Americans (who have lived there for thousands of years, but were pushed off their lands by European settlers) used opened clam shells to scrape away the dirty bits. People living in Hawaii and the Caribbean sometimes preferred wiping with the hairy husks of coconuts. In Japan, going back many centuries, small wooden scraping sticks called *chūgi* were very common – they were a bit like the sticks you get with an ice lolly. And when the ancient Greeks went to the potty, 2,500 years ago, they used smoothed-off bits of broken pottery called *pessoi*.

For roughly the past 1,400 years, many Muslims have followed the guidance in the sacred Hadiths (the written sayings of the Prophet) which says to wipe with an odd number of smooth pebbles, if there is no water. These days, many prefer to clean themselves with water poured from what looks like a small watering can (often called an *aftabeh*, *lota* or *bodna*). They wash themselves with the left hand, as the right is for eating food. In fact, many people around the world think it's super gross that people like me use toilet paper, and don't instead wash our bottoms immediately. At least I don't share my used toilet paper with strangers, like the Romans!

Ooh, I'll take the hairy husks!

GREG'S GREATEST

TOILET PAPER JOKE

Other really common wiping materials throughout history were moss, leaves, hay, straw and other plant material. This stuff is always freely available, so you can see why it was used all the way back to the Stone Age. In fact, here is a genuine joke from 500 years ago: "What is the cleanest leaf in the forest? Holly, because nobody dares use it to wipe their backside!"

OUCH!

4 SHOWER

If you're anything like me, you like to start your day with a nice shower – the gushing water kickstarts my sluggish morning brain, and helps me smell less disgusting for when I'm meeting other people. Showers are hygienic, convenient, and they make great karaoke venues if you like singing to yourself very loudly (apologies to my neighbours...). What's not to love?

THE FIRST SHOWER

The first modern shower was invented by a Brit called William Feetham in 1767. He built a tall, thin cubicle with a bathtub at the bottom, and a bucket at the top which could be overturned by yanking a chain. But the really clever thing was the bucket automatically refilled itself thanks to a hydraulic pump that sucked up the water in the bathtub, meaning there was no need for a servant to keep fetching buckets of water.

However, there were downsides. The water was chilly. Oh, and it would get dirty! The user was eventually just sploshing around in their own filthy, sweaty juice which kept being recycled by the pump and sploshed all over their face. Gross! Also, the cubicle was sometimes mounted on little wheels so it could be moved around the house. Perfectly sensible … unless, of course, someone forgot to lock the wheels in place. In which case they might find themselves rolling naked down the corridor!

DICKENS' DEMON!

The people who bought William Feetham's portable shower probably didn't mind washing in cold water, as it was very fashionable at the time. Even a century later, the famous Victorian novelist Charles Dickens had a very, very cold shower installed in his bathroom. The shower was so powerful and noisy that his family called it "The Demon"! Dickens believed that washing in very cold water was good for you, and made you physically strong – the Victorians called this *hydrotherapy*. Personally, I can't think of anything worse. I love ridiculously hot showers and baths that make me turn bright pink like a boiled lobster.

It was actually the Victorians who invented the modern bathroom I'm used to washing in. Before they turned up, washing was done in the bedroom or even the kitchen. After all, Mr Feetham's portable shower wasn't connected to any pipes, and so could go anywhere in the house. But wealthy Victorians began demanding a special room for their washing and toilet facilities. By the 1870s, the bathroom could not only be plumbed into a permanent water supply, but that water could also be heated by the kitchen stove, or a specialist boiler. At last, people could have hot showers! Unfortunately, the Victorians weren't particularly keen on health and safety, and sometimes the water would be so hot that people were horribly burned. So, when you have your shower, consider yourself very lucky that you're not a Victorian…

GREEKS DIDN'T REEK

In ancient societies, washing was very important. The rich might wash their own bodies, or perhaps order their enslaved servant to do all the scrubbing. We know wealthy ancient Greeks did both, 2,500 years ago.

But the Greeks also had public bathhouses – called *balaneion* – where lots of people could gather together to wash. These were impressive buildings that had some of the oldest ever shower nozzles, and they also had underfloor heating technology called *hypokauston* (Greek for "beneath-burn") – more on this invention later! This also warmed the pools for bathers to splosh round in. However, some Greeks – most notably the mega-macho Spartans – hated warm-water luxury and wanted everyone to know how hardcore they were. Yes, Spartans chose to wash in cold water. Perhaps they would have enjoyed Dickens' Demon shower?

GREG'S GREATEST

RIDICULOUS INVENTION

Surely the funniest shower in history was the *velo-douche* (that's French for "pedal-shower"), which was invented in the 1890s. How did it work? Well, the nozzle was connected to a water pump, and that was connected to an exercise bike. The faster you pedalled, the more water was pumped onto your head. It was genius! Or was it ludicrous? On the one hand, we all need a bit of exercise, don't we? But, on the other hand, didn't people get sweaty while they were trying to get clean? The velo-douche was a bit weird, but I love it!

SHAMPOO

There have been many ways to wash hair in the past. One popular way was for people to crack an egg on their head, and rub it into their hair and scalp to clean away dirt. I guess that would make them egg-heads, right? When we wash our hair in the shower, we call it shampooing – which is a fantastically fun word to say aloud. But did you know that shampoo has a fascinating history that owes a lot to just one man?

THE SHAMPOO SURGEON

Sheikh din Muhammad was born in Patna, India in 1759. Back then, a powerful British business, called the East India Company, was taking control of India through trade and taxes. In fact, it had its own armies and hired local Indian soldiers, called *sepoys*. Muhammad joined up and learned many skills before leaving India for ever. He went to Ireland, then to London, where a man named Basil Cochrane was setting up traditional Indian baths to help people relax and recover from illness. Muhammad said, "Hire me! I'm from India, and I know stuff!" So, Cochrane did.

What's this got to do with washing your hair? Well, our word *shampoo* comes from the Hindi word *chāmpo*, for the traditional art of Indian body and head massages. Muhammad brought these ancient skills to London and the baths were a great success. Great news, right? Nope! Other bathhouses stole their idea.

You might need to remove your crown, Your Majesty...

Muhammad moved to the seaside town of Brighton, where all the royals and rich people went to recuperate after a long year of being posh. He changed his name to Sake Dean Mahomet and opened his own fancy new baths. He also gave himself a job title, "shampooing surgeon", which sounded so impressive that even the king became a loyal customer! It's thanks to Muhammad that the word *shampoo* became so common in the English language. Nice one, Mr Muhammad!

6 SOAP

Of course, when we hop into the shower and begin our noisy karaoke session, we don't expect to get properly squeaky clean just by standing under the water. No, we also use cleaning products to banish the smells, bacteria and dirt. The simplest of these is soap, but you might be surprised to learn not everybody in history used it.

SCRAPY, NOT SOAPY

strigil

If you'd been a Roman citizen, the most likely way you'd have cleaned your body would have been with a bronze scraping tool called a *strigil.* Sounds painful!

The strigil was a very simple bit of kit. Its long, thin, curved blade was used to scrape the dirt and dead skin from a person's body. However, the crucial ingredient was olive oil. Now we use it for cooking, but the Romans would rub it onto their bodies – the dirt and sweat would get mixed up into a slippery layer that could be scraped off.

And you'll never guess what the sticky, dirty, oily scrapings (called *strigimentum*) were used for. It was … medicine. YUCK! According to the famous ancient writer Pliny the Elder, doctors recommended patients apply other people's sweaty scrapings to their sore bits. Gladiator sweat was also sold to people who wanted to feel young and healthy. For this reason, the scrapings from gymnasiums and gladiator arenas were worth lots of money. I guess you could say the dealers were *scraping* a living…

Ah, yes, you need some strigimentum – don't worry, Felix is the sweatiest man I know!

THE GORY STORY OF SOAP

Soap was possibly invented 4,500 years ago by Sumerian people in Iraq. They took ashes from burned wood and soaked them in water to make lye. Scientists call this mixture sodium hydroxide, and it is NASTY! It burns the skin and can even blind you. Obviously, that makes it a terrible soap to use in the shower. The Sumerians only used it for washing clothes.

It wasn't until maybe 1,300 years ago that soap for smelly humans came along. The city of Aleppo, in Syria, became famous for making luxurious green bars of soap with olive oil and vegetable fats, which didn't burn the skin. But how did this become popular with rich Europeans? Sadly, it's a horrible story. In 1095, the Pope (the leader of the Catholic Church) called for a "Crusade". This was a religious war fought over who got to control the Holy Land of the Middle East, which is sacred to Christians, Muslims and Jews. There were many nasty, violent Crusades. While fighting in Syria, the European soldiers saw the green soap made in Aleppo, and brought it back to Spain. There it changed into a white bar called Castile soap.

New burn-free recipe!

GREG'S GREATEST

SOAP-SELLING STUNTS

In 1807, English hairdresser Andrew Pears invented a bar of soap that became very popular. After he died, his company did even better because it was run by Thomas J. Barratt, who understood the power of advertising.

Pears had previously used shockingly racist adverts, and Barratt did the same. But his most famous idea was decorating soap packets with a beautiful painting of a boy blowing bubbles. He also did publicity stunts, sponsored celebrities and put the Pears logo on coins to give away. This led to modern advertising. Ever wonder why some TV shows are called "soap operas"? They were sponsored by soap companies, who wanted millions of people to see their adverts!

23

7 UNDERWEAR

Once you've dried off from your shower, the obvious next stage is to pop on some clothes, otherwise breakfast with your family is going to be *really* awkward. I'd guess the first item you reach for is a trusty pair of underpants. Wise choice! But, for something so simple, pants have a surprisingly complicated history.

A LOAD OF OLD PANTS

When British Egyptologist Howard Carter and his Egyptian team broke into the tomb of Pharaoh Tutankhamun in 1922, they found 5,000 astonishing objects. But do you know what my absolute fave discovery was? It was King Tut's undercrackers! Yes, he was buried with 145 spare pairs of pants, which boggles my brain. Who needs that many if they're dead? Didn't they believe in a laundry service in the Egyptian afterlife? Were royal pants sacred because they had touched King Tut's sacred body, so his servants couldn't throw them away?! I have SO MANY questions!

Ancient Egyptian undies weren't like ours. King Tut's were basically a linen nappy made of two triangles, held in place by string or a belt at the sides. He then wore a linen skirt over the top. But, around the world, many people wore similar breechcloths – and not as underwear, but as outerwear! When we look at images of Aztecs, who lived in Mexico over 500 years ago, some men are only wearing a breechcloth. Is it still underwear if it's not under anything? I feel like that's cheating!

SWEATY OR SHIVERY

The Romans called their underpants *subligacula*. We know soldiers and gladiators wore them in battle, but we don't know much about what ordinary Romans popped on under their tunics, togas and dresses. Maybe nothing? It was pretty warm in most of the Roman Empire, so maybe they didn't need it. Indeed, in colder places, like Scandinavia and Britain, medieval people wore baggy shorts (*braies*) under their tunics to keep their legs warm.

BLOUSES AND BUM-FLAPS

By the 1800s, however, people in Europe were deffo wearing underwear – but it was waaaay bigger than yours! Girls and ladies might wear baggy knee-length shorts, called *drawers*, plus a *chemise blouse*, or they might combine the two into a single garment called *pantaloons* or *knickerbockers*. Men could wear an even bigger onesie called a *combination* or *union suit*, which usually covered everything from neck to ankle. Of course, there's nothing worse than desperately needing the toilet and having to totally strip off first. So the union suit had a cunning bum-flap that allowed a chap to have a poo while keeping his kecks on. Cheeky!

In Europe and North America, underwear design changed a huge amount between the 1800s and 1960s, and it wasn't until the 1930s that our familiar modern briefs were invented. Sadly, the hilarious bum-flap did not survive the journey. Booo!

SO fashionable!

SOCK IT TO ME

Your underwear probably also includes a pair of socks. When I was growing up, I was told it was a terrible fashion crime to wear socks with sandals. But we now know that ancient Egyptians, Romans and Greeks all did exactly this! They had a special sock that was split in two, like a camel's hoof, so the sandal strap could slide between the middle toes. This was similar to a type of traditional sock, called *tabi*, worn in Japan.

In Europe, socks mostly started small in ancient times, then got longer and longer until they became stockings (or a pair of tights) in the 1400s. Then, in the 1800s, they shortened all the way back down again, when men started wearing long trousers. So, the story of the sock is quite literally one of many ups and downs!

Belongs to GREG JENNER

FITS TO A TEE

Finally, you might be surprised to learn that your favourite T-shirt would have been considered underwear not so long ago. Do you remember those union suits with the bum-flaps from the 1800s? Well, sometimes factory workers got hot in them, so they cut them in half, leaving just the top part.

By the early 1900s, the American navy made just the top section part of a sailor's uniform. This was widely copied by ordinary people, who wore it under their shirt, but rarely as a layer of clothing that others could see. It was only when Marlon Brando – a very famous movie star – wore a T-shirt in an iconic film called *A Streetcar Named Desire* in 1951 and people thought he looked SOOOOO COOOOOOL, that the T-shirt was turned from embarrassing underwear into the symbol of rock 'n' roll rebellion. Nice!

Gee whiz!

Soooooo coooool!

Rock 'n' roll!

WOW!

Amazing!

CLOTHES

With underwear on, next comes the rest of your outfit – otherwise you'll be going to school in just your pants and socks, and that's literally the stuff of nightmares! Most clothing serves three purposes: it keeps us warm, it stops us being naked in public (awkward!), and it's there to be seen by others. The first two are just us being sensible, but that last one is what we call fashion. It's where the thing you wear is an expression of who you want other people to think you are. This can be a big deal. Oh, and speaking of which...

THE FASHION POLICE

These days, we can wear whatever we like, provided we can afford it. But in medieval times, so-called Sumptuary Laws restricted certain fabrics and colours to only the most important people. Seven hundred years ago, King Edward III of England said only a knight or noble got to wear velvet, and only royals could show off in gold, silver or purple. Why purple? It was thanks to the ancient Romans! It was their royal colour because getting purple dye was super hard work. It had to be squeezed from a special type of sea-snail that lived in the waters near Tyre (in modern Lebanon), so it was very expensive. Oh, and did you know? Modern purple dye was invented by accident in 1856 when a young scientist, William Henry Perkin, was trying to make a medicine! Talk about a colourful history...

NO PURPLE

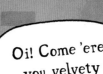
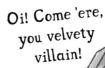

Oi! Come 'ere, you velvety villain!

THE NO-FUN SHOGUN

Another ruler to bring in clothing laws was the shogun of Japan, Tokugawa Tsunayoshi. In 1681 he was outraged after he had a lovely chat with a beautifully dressed lady, thinking she was from a high-status family, only to learn she was just a merchant's wife whose husband had grown rich selling stuff. To avoid more embarrassment, the shogun banned merchants from wearing ornately designed, short-sleeved robes (called *kosode*), and restricted them to simple *iki kosode* robes instead. Of course, people just ignored him! They hid the fancy robes under their simple ones, and flashed them to their friends in private. Sneaky!

That outfit is criminal!

Thanks!

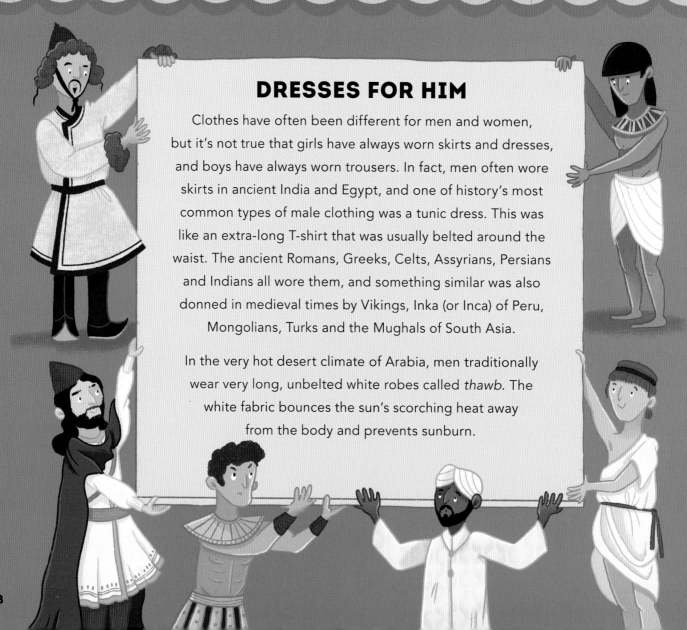

DRESSES FOR HIM

Clothes have often been different for men and women, but it's not true that girls have always worn skirts and dresses, and boys have always worn trousers. In fact, men often wore skirts in ancient India and Egypt, and one of history's most common types of male clothing was a tunic dress. This was like an extra-long T-shirt that was usually belted around the waist. The ancient Romans, Greeks, Celts, Assyrians, Persians and Indians all wore them, and something similar was also donned in medieval times by Vikings, Inka (or Inca) of Peru, Mongolians, Turks and the Mughals of South Asia.

In the very hot desert climate of Arabia, men traditionally wear very long, unbelted white robes called *thawb*. The white fabric bounces the sun's scorching heat away from the body and prevents sunburn.

TROUSERS FOR HER

Trousers have a long global history. Baggy ones called *sirwal* have been very common for more than a thousand years in South Asia and the Middle East, and were worn by lads and ladies. In Japan, wide trousers for men and women are traditionally called *hakama*. But trousers only became fashionable in Europe and North America around 200 years ago, and they were just for men. When women tried to wear them in the mid-1800s, it caused a HUGE kerfuffle!

Avoiding the fireplace is the hottest new trend.

Amelia Bloomer was an American women's rights campaigner, who found tight corsets and heavy skirts to be unfairly restrictive compared to men's comfy clothes. Amelia started wearing big, baggy Turkish trousers under short dresses, which were nicknamed "bloomers" in her honour. Alas, the sight of ladies in trousers made some men EXPLODE with pouty rage (they didn't actually explode, they just went very red in the face)! Bloomers didn't succeed. Instead, in came crinolines (a hidden cage under the skirt that made it fan out like a tent). Crinolines were lighter (yay!) but also easily caught fire (yikes!) if a lady got too close to the fireplace. You can see why women wanted trousers!

It took another 30 years for ladies to win the battle and pop on their slacks. And even then they had to be playing sport or riding a bike (because then it was Official Safety Clothing, you see?). It wasn't until the 1920s that it became cool for fashionable ladies to wear long trousers, made by famous designers like Coco Chanel. It's a bit silly that European and American men weren't allowed dresses, and women weren't allowed trousers, when everywhere else in the world both had been totally normal for aaaaages!

Safety first!

GLASSES

Once you're wearing your clothes, you might also need to pop in some contact lenses or put on some glasses – not least in case you've done what I often do, and put your clothes on back-to-front!

You might not look at a pair of specs and think, "Wow, that's so high-tech!" But, actually, the medical field of *optometry* (looking after people's eyes) has a very long and complicated history, and glasses are part of that. So, when did they first turn up?

I CAN SEE!

Surprisingly, spectacles date back to medieval Italy. Our earliest written reference is from the 1280s, and then a bit later we find paintings and *illuminated manuscripts* (a fancy phrase for medieval books with hand-drawn pictures) showing people wearing chunky glasses over both eyes. The frames for these specs were made of wood, bone, leather and other natural products, but they didn't have handles that slid over the ears.

No, they were held in place by a little bridge that pinched the nose, so maybe they weren't too comfy to wear for long spells? Also, we know they fell off sometimes, because archaeologists once found a pair of wooden specs in a medieval toilet! I guess if you lose your glasses, it's hard to find them again. Then again, if they land in a big old pile of poo, maybe you don't want to find them…

Oh, and spectacles weren't just for making tiny, scribbly handwriting bigger. You can grind glass into the ideal shape to correct vision problems, such as short-sightedness (where you can only see nearby things). Medieval people knew eyesight worsens as we get older: in 1466, the Duke of Milan bulk-ordered a variety of lenses to prepare for this. Smart chap!

I'll take them ALL!

BRILLIANT BEN'S BIFOCALS

The American inventor Benjamin Franklin struggled with a common vision problem called *presbyopia*. In 1784, he wrote about how he kept having to swap one set of glasses, for seeing people's faces, with another set of specs for looking down at his dinner. Either his friends were blurry or his food was, and the constant specs-swapping was annoying.

So Franklin invented a pair of glasses called *bifocals*, which combined two types of lenses. The top half of each lens was for seeing faraway, and the bottom was for reading and spotting his food. This invention was so good, they are still used today. Nice one, Ben!

GREG'S GREATEST

SUNGLASSES
(WITHOUT THE GLASS)

Indigenous peoples of the icy Arctic north – such as the Inuit in Canada and Greenland, and the Yup'ik, Iñupiat and Athabaskan in Alaska – traditionally don't wear sunglasses. Instead, they have protected their eyes by wearing goggles (made of wood, whalebone or caribou hoof) with small slits cut into them. This stops the sun's glare bouncing off the ice and harming their eyesight.

A COOL PAIR OF SHADES

Even if your eyesight is pretty good, I reckon you've probably got a pair of sunglasses for the summertime (I live in the UK, so I only get to wear mine roughly three times per year...). As well as protecting us from the sun's glare, shades are now associated with looking cool and glamorous. In fact, some celebs wear them indoors, because they think it makes them look mysterious and unapproachable.

However, wearing tinted glasses to look mysterious actually dates back 750 years to medieval China. Judges in legal trials wore *ai dai*, which were smoky spectacles of quartz crystal. These stopped people guessing if the judge thought someone was guilty or not. Maybe they also allowed a sleepy judge to take a nap without anyone knowing!

JEWELLERY BOX

Now, how about accessorising your outfit? At your age, I certainly couldn't afford shiny bling, but I liked wearing a colourful wristwatch. Of course, wearing jewellery is nothing new, though sometimes these accessories had other uses besides looking nice...

MAGICAL PROTECTION

In ancient Egypt, it was common for people to wear an object called an *amulet* (actually a later Roman word), which they hoped was chock-full of magic to protect them from evil spells, bad luck or poor health. Amulets were often made from a bluey-green glazed pottery called *faience*, and they were shaped to look like the powerful Egyptian gods, or the animals famously associated with the gods, such as snakes, frogs, rams, elephants and scarab beetles.

Among the most popular amulets was a necklace or pendant in the shape of the Eye of Horus. Horus was the falcon-headed god whose eye had been ripped out in a fight with the evil god Seth, but it had regrown thanks to another god's help. Egyptians thought wearing his eye would help them recover from all sorts of injuries.

Not all ancient jewellery was magical. Ancient Egyptian women sometimes wore little crescent moons and metal bells on their ankles, so they jingled when they walked. They must have sounded lovely!

VICTORIAN JEWELLERY FADS

In the Victorian era in Britain, people were fascinated by nature – probably because cities were becoming so big and dirty that they wanted to remember what the countryside was like. This led to the most extraordinary fashion in the 1860s for women's jewellery made from actual dead insects! Yes, the wings and bodies of beetles, butterflies, fireflies, weevils and moths were fastened to rare flowers and then made into necklaces, earrings, brooches and hairpins.

GREG'S GREATEST

CLASSY COPROLITES

An even stranger Victorian trend was *coprolite* jewellery – beautifully polished stones that were tens of millions of years old. What were the stones made of? Well, coprolite comes from the ancient Greek words *kopros* (dung) and *lithos* (stone). Yup, glamorous people had fossilised dinosaur poo dangling from their ears. Charming!

BLING RINGS THAT DID THINGS

You sign your name with a pen, right? In medieval Europe, kings and powerful lords used a special signet ring with their personal emblem etched into the metal. Wax was heated, so it went all gloopy, and then the ring was pushed down to squish their emblem into the hot wax. Once it dried, this seal showed a document was official.

A much sillier ring was owned by the wife of a Russian ambassador. In 1768, she sat down to dinner next to the French ambassador, the Duc de Guînes, who everyone hated because he was a show-off. She was wearing a special squirt-ring, and when he leaned in to look at it, she squirted him in the eye with water! He laughed, but she did it twice more, so he chucked a glass of wine in her face! Talk about awkward…

MIRROR

11

I'm not a big fan of mirrors, because my face resembles a cross between a cowardly lion and a confused weasel. But I suppose mirrors are useful, and, before you head off to school, you might need a quick glance to check if you have toothpaste smeared all over your chin... (I do this all the time!)

ANCIENT LOOKERS

The word *mirror* comes from the Latin (Roman language) word *mirare* – meaning "to look at" – but mirrors are even older than the Romans! The earliest mirrors are from 8,000 years ago, in the world's oldest town, called Çatalhöyük, in Turkey. Here, several Stone Age women were found buried with polished black mirrors made of a type of glass called *obsidian*, which is produced by lava from mega-hot volcanoes cooling very quickly. How cool is that? I mean … quite literally!

Somewhere around 5,000 to 4,000 years ago, mirrors also popped up in Bronze Age Egypt and China. By then, they were made of polished copper, because humans had figured out how to use metals. These ancient mirrors weren't whopping great things hanging on the wall. They were dinky hand-held objects that curved slightly to give a better close-up of the face – ideal for putting on make-up or shaving.

And it wasn't just metal that could be polished. 1,900 years ago, a notorious Roman emperor called Domitian became totally convinced people were trying to murder him (in fairness, emperors got murdered A LOT!). So he had the walls of his palace lined with a shiny mineral called *phengite*, so he could spot the reflections of any potential assassins. Clever!

WHO'S THERE?

HALL OF MIRRORS

Of course, you probably think a mirror is made of glass. So, when did that turn up? Glass dates back at least 5,400 years, but it wasn't used in mirrors until about 2,000 years ago, in the Middle Eastern region we now call Lebanon. This glass was rough and murky, with a blueish tinge, so not great for checking yourself out. Our modern mirrors arrived in the 1400s, during the Renaissance, when craftspeople learned how to blow even, flat, uncracked panes of silvered glass.

The best glass came from the Venetian island of Murano, in Italy. Other countries wanted to steal Venice's glassmakers, so Venice offered them tax cuts, cash, the chance to marry nobles' daughters and a job for life, provided they stayed put. If they tried to leave, they and their families were arrested for treason, or murdered. Crikey, who knew mirrors could be so valuable!

Personally, I think the most glorious example of Venetian mirrors is in the Palace of Versailles, in France. Its hall was made for King Louis XIV in 1684, and it boasts 357 mirrors in a massive room 73 metres long. Though King Louis was determined to only hire French workers, his architect knew that the best glassworkers were Venetians, so he hired a few. Sensible move!

Oi! You're not allowed to leave!

GREG'S GREATEST

MIRROR-SMASHING ACCIDENT!

In the 1760s, there lived a cunning musician and inventor from Belgium called John-Joseph Merlin. His best invention, I reckon, was roller skates. Merlin was a bit of a show-off, and he was invited to entertain the posh guests at a big London party. He whizzed around on his skates, while playing his violin, but he'd forgotten to invent brakes. Unfortunately, our brilliant Belgian hurtled at great speed into a massive, expensive mirror, smashing it into smithereens and hurting himself quite badly in the process. Oops!

HAIR GEL

While you're looking in the mirror, maybe you check your hair. Hair keeps growing, even when we're snoozing – it's very sneaky like that – so some days I go to bed with nice hair but wake up to discover a rat's nest on my head! How we style our hair (or don't) says a lot about us to others. This isn't new. And throughout history, hair has been styled in loads of different ways.

THE PEAT-BOG PUNK

In 2003, workmen in Ireland discovered an Iron Age body in a peat bog. Scientific tests showed he was a young man who'd been sacrificed about 2,300 years ago – a nasty end to his short life – but more surprising was that he had a punktastic hairstyle, shaved at the front then styled up high on top with hair gel. Incredibly, it wasn't even locally produced hair gel! No, it was made of plant oil and pine tree resin, imported from France or Spain. Was he a fancy fella buying foreign beauty supplies? Or was it smeared on his head as part of the sacrifice?

Scientists studying Egyptian mummies from 3,500 years ago have also found that rich Egyptians styled their hair with animal grease, so it kept its shape in life and in death.

GREG'S WORST

HAIRCARE ADVICE

The haircare tip that I never, ever think you should try is from Renaissance Italy, about 500 years ago. It was fashionable for women to have high foreheads. They didn't just shave the front of their heads, they also smeared that patch of skin in a paste made from pig fat, berries, mustard, boiled swallows and – the secret ingredient – cat poo blended with vinegar. It apparently stopped hair growing back, although maybe it stopped their friends coming back too. Urgh!

BEAR BEWARE!

In Victorian Britain, the most popular type of hair-setting pomade for men was made of bear grease. Well, sort of... You see, bears were quite rare, so dodgy manufacturers would cheat and use pig grease instead, mixed with perfume. This meant that some Victorian chaps probably smelled like a cross between a bouquet of flowers and a sausage sandwich. To stop customers getting suspicious, merchants would sometimes have a bear skin hanging in the shop, to pretend they'd just killed one. Naughty!

WIG OUT!

In the mid-1600s, King Louis XIV of France and King Charles II of England were trendsetters who wore long, curly wigs that made them look like poodles. But fashions change! By the early 1700s, the popular *ramillies* wig was much shorter, and had a long, plaited ponytail. By the 1770s, it was fashionable for a chap to use white powder on his wig, and to stash his ponytail inside a velvet bag, which hung off the back of his neck. That would be like keeping part of your hair in your schoolbag while it's still attached to your head!

Posh European women in the 1700s didn't wear full wigs. Instead, they combined their real hair with fake extensions to create amazingly high hairstyles called a *pouf*. These piled up on top of their heads, supported by pins and hidden metal scaffolds, to resemble a massive, tiered wedding cake made of hair. It was fashionable to pin fruit, fabrics, feathers and ornaments into the pouf as a way of showing off. Queen Marie Antoinette of France was famous for her huge headdresses, including the *coiffure au jardiniere*, which was like a mini vegetable garden on her head!

Such fashion icons also styled their hair to reflect the latest news. When the French navy defeated the British in battle, French ladies wore battleships in their hair! I guess the next time you do well in a school test, you could stick the evidence on your head? Just tell people it was VERY cool in the 1700s.

I got my wig in the SAIL.

It's the HEIGHT of fashion!

CEREAL

It's long been said that breakfast is the most important meal of the day. However, we don't know much about what many people ate for breakfast before the 1600s. For many Europeans, it was maybe just a bit of bread and cheese. My breakfast of choice is now porridge with honey and sliced banana, but when I was your age, I was all about the sugary breakfast cereals, which tasted great but left me hungry an hour later (that's the problem with sugar!). But did you know these cereals were pretty much invented by accident? And even putting milk on them came about by chance?

GOT MILK?

Your breakfast cereal is going to taste a bit dry if you don't pour milk on top. Actually, roughly 65% of the world's population can't do that, because milk makes them feel unwell. Why? Here comes the science chat!

It all goes back to the Neolithic era (Late Stone Age), about 11,000 years ago. In this period, people settled down in villages and towns, particularly in the region we now call Turkey, and started to keep animals for meat, milk, wool and other useful things. However, most people couldn't drink the animal milk without feeling horribly queasy and farty. Those rare ones who could had, purely by chance, inherited a genetic mutation that let their bodies produce an enzyme called *lactase*. I'm afraid it wasn't the sort of mutation that gave them *X-Men* superhero powers – lactase basically breaks down the natural sugars in milk, and so stops all that nasty build-up of tummy gases.

These people passed the mutation on to their kids, and it kept being passed down through the generations, until gradually it spread around the world. But there are large parts of the world, such as China, where most of the population lack the lactase enzyme, and so milk is not a big part of the diet.

THE KELLOGGS DEBATE

In the 1870s, there was a famous doctor in Michigan, USA, called John Harvey Kellogg. He ran a health spa that was visited by all sorts of patients, including celebrities and presidents. John believed that people's salty, fatty, meaty diets were making them unwell, so he told people to be vegetarian and eat nothing spicy. Pretty sensible advice, right? Well ... on top of this, he offered various treatments – some of them a bit weird, to be honest.

IIIIII feeeelllll aaaaa biiiittt siiiiick!

36 ... 37 ...

These included yoghurt squirted up the bum, electrocution, constant bathing in water, chewing each mouthful of food 40 times and vibrating chairs that shook people until their bunged-up bowels loosened. (Safety warning: do not try any of these! Well, I guess the chewing isn't dangerous, but it's still super boring!)

John and his brother Will Keith Kellogg started experimenting with creating a pre-prepared breakfast meal that was easy to mass-produce. They started with hard-baked rolls, but a woman broke her teeth on them! Not great. Next, they ground the rolls up into little nuggets. Still not great! And then finally, after lots of experiments, Will invented wheat flakes, which could be eaten with milk.

First they called it Granula, but changed it to Granola when another inventor complained that was his brand name. These breakfast battles got pretty intense, with over 100 rival cereals available! But the Kelloggs cleverly switched recipe to corn, which was cheaper and tastier.

Big success brought big brotherly bickering. Will was a great businessman, and started his own famous company – Kelloggs – in 1906. John got jealous and launched his own rival Kelloggs brand! Furious, they sued each other for control of their famous surname. In the end, Will became extremely rich, and gave lots of cash to charity, but the brothers never spoke again!

TOOTHBRUSH

What does your toothbrush look like? Mine is electric, which makes my nose tingle when it buzzes in my mouth. Many people use a manual toothbrush, which is moulded plastic with bristles. Since 1938, these bristles have often been made of nylon, a type of special, very soft plastic.

Plastic toothbrushes are meant to be replaced every four months, so a person might chuck away 200 in their lifetime! Sadly, plastic doesn't *biodegrade* (meaning it doesn't get broken down by bacteria, like natural products). Instead, all that plastic ends up polluting the oceans, or in rubbish dumps. That's why some designers are asking if we can learn from the old ways of brushing our teeth. But what were they?

THE MISWAK

We know that people in the Late Stone Age, 9,000 years ago, did basic dentistry – if you had toothache, someone might have drilled little holes in your painful teeth with a bow-drill used for punching holes in jewellery beads. Even better, they might have then given you fillings made of beeswax! Impressive stuff from people who hadn't even invented the wheel yet. But did they clean their teeth? We just don't know! Alas, the furthest back we can confidently go is to the Bronze Age, about 5,500 years ago, in ancient Mesopotamia (modern Iraq). We know these clever people used a soft stick from a particular tree, which they frayed at the ends by chewing on it, creating a natural type of brush. Smart!

Avoid dentistry, chew a dentist tree!

Hundreds of millions of people around the world still do this today. This natural brush is called a *miswak*, and many people who live in South Asia, the Middle East and large parts of Africa chew a miswak stick taken from the *Salvadora persica* tree. This tree produces a natural chemical that helps to fight off bacteria. A miswak can harm the gums if you brush too hard, but careful use helps protect the teeth from plaque and decay. Ancient traditions can be just as good as modern technology sometimes.

A BRUSH WITH THE LAW

So who invented toothbrushes? We can start, as we so often do, with the medieval Chinese. They started using brushes during the Tang Dynasty, around 1,200 years ago. These toothbrushes were made from very stiff bristles taken from pigs, and that same material was also used when the toothbrush was introduced into Europe in the late 1700s. But the man who did this didn't know about Chinese toothbrushes! His name was William Addis and I suppose he invented the toothbrush for a second time. But he wasn't some boffin beavering away in his lab. No, he was banged up in a London jail!

We're not sure what naughty crime Addis had committed, but while he sat in prison, he took a pig bone from his dinner, drilled some holes in it, and then inserted the bristles from either the same pig, or from a broom in the jail cell. Hey presto – he'd invented the toothbrush (again)! Addis founded a company to sell them, and it's still going today, but other people weren't so keen on his super-stiff pig bristles. Instead, they preferred badger fur or horsehair, which were much softer (though not as good at removing plaque). And lots of people didn't bother with brushes at all; they carried on with the earlier European tradition of cleaning their teeth with rags, toothpicks and metal sticks.

Hmm, bit big... I think I need a mini mouth broom!

FRESH HORSE HAIR BRUSHES SOLD HERE

FALSE TEETH

The truth is that before the 1900s, many people had bad teeth, to the point that they actually fell out. Sometimes, lack of oral hygiene was the cause. And sometimes, it was TOO MUCH oral hygiene that bashed and battered the teeth. If people had spent years poking around with metal sticks and stiff pig bristles … well, the human mouth wasn't really designed for all that punishment.

So, it's also worth mentioning the history of false teeth. In the 1700s, in Europe and North America, rich people sometimes bought fake teeth carved from animal bone and ivory. Knowing that nice teeth were important for getting a husband, some young ladies had their real teeth pulled out and replaced with false ones as an eighteenth birthday present – horrible! I'd much prefer an Xbox…

But now things get more grim. It was also quite common to buy "Waterloo teeth" extracted from the mouths of soldiers killed in battle (such as at the Battle of Waterloo in 1815). Horrid! But it wasn't just the dead who suffered this; poor people sometimes had to trade their own teeth just to afford food and shelter. A horrible choice to have to make.

Tragically, some people had no choice at all. When America's famous first president, George Washington, ordered a French dentist to make him some false teeth, historians think some of those teeth were probably ripped out of the mouths of the poor Black people Mr Washington kept enslaved. These people had no rights and no say over what happened to their bodies. Horrifying, isn't it?

TOOTHPASTE

Brushing teeth is great, but if you want to polish your teeth to a shiny shade of white then you need toothpaste too. Mine is minty fresh, hardens my tooth enamel and foams in my mouth. This is all thanks to a blend of different ingredients, mixed together by clever scientists. But toothpaste has a much longer history than you might expect...

SALTY SMILES

Toothpaste might be 5,000 years old. Apparently, ancient Egyptians cleaned their teeth with a mixture of ashes, burned eggshells, pumice stone and myrrh (for a nice smell!). But what about minty fresh toothpaste? Well, another Egyptian recipe from 1,700 years ago blended rock salt, pepper, mint leaves and the roots of an iris flower. These paste combos worked by grinding the jagged, grainy stuff – the salt, pumice and eggshells – against the tooth enamel, helping to polish it. Meanwhile, the herbal flavours freshened the breath. Not bad!

Something similar was still being recommended nearly 800 years ago by the important medieval doctor Gilbertus Anglicus (a fancy Latin name that meant Gilbert the Englishman). He recommended chewing the mixture for a while and then swallowing it, whereas you're not meant to swallow modern toothpaste. Salty toothpaste was being used on the other side of the world too, in medieval China, where they also made a paste from a type of spongy mushroom called *poria*. Not so much minty fresh as fungus fresh!

POLISH YOUR PEARLY WHITES

If your smile was looking less than sparkly white, there were a few brightening techniques available. In Roman times, posh people had their teeth polished with powdered antler from a stag! But if a person couldn't catch a stag (they're pretty big and scary!), I suppose they could have tried a medieval recipe that said:

> "… take walnut shells well cleaned of the green interior rind … rub the teeth three times a day, and when they have been well rubbed … wash the mouth with warm wine, and with salt mixed in if desired."

Because people didn't have toothbrushes in Europe yet, the cleaning mixture was applied to the teeth with a linen cloth.

Where am I going to find a stag?

WASH YOUR MOUTH OUT WITH SOAP!

The 1800s was when companies in Britain and North America started advertising tooth-cleaning powders and *dentifrices* in newspapers. There were lots of types, but one of the most popular recipes was a mix of charcoal and honey that people rubbed onto their teeth and gums. In fairness, charcoal is very *abrasive* (meaning it scrubs the surface well), so it probably did get rid of dirt, but it also would have damaged teeth in the long run. And the honey wouldn't have helped much either – sugar causes dental decay!

GREG'S GREATEST

TOOTH-WHITENING DISASTER

In Victorian times, some dentists whitened teeth using types of acid, but this was very dangerous. If the wrong acid was used, or if the right one was left on for too long, the patient's teeth could be totally destroyed. The poor patient would be in agony and the ravaged teeth would have to be yanked out with pliers! MEGA OUCH!

Are you sure this works?

Obviously!

44

A BEAUTIFUL BLACKENED SMILE

However, just because most people through history have valued white teeth, it doesn't mean it was the same around the world. In many cultures of South-East Asia, such as in Vietnam, Thailand and Nepal, people instead blackened their teeth. Perhaps the most famous tradition was in Japan, lasting from medieval times until about 100 years ago, where tar-black teeth were a sign of beauty for a fancy Japanese lady.

This custom was called *ohaguro*. It was done by damaging the tooth enamel by eating acidic foods, like loads of lemon. After this, the lady would paint her teeth with a thick potion made of rice wine, water, vinegar, spices, copper and iron.

Why did posh Japanese ladies do this? Well, they believed it kept teeth healthy, plus it contrasted impactfully with their white make-up, tinted eyebrows and red-powdered cheeks. Foreign visitors found it deeply shocking, so it fell out of favour in Japan, but tooth-blackening still happens in some parts of the world today.

FRESH BREATH

As well as wanting teeth to look cleaner (or blacker, whichever people preferred), most people also wanted their breath to smell nice – there's nothing worse than kissing someone with rotten breath! Across the world, lots of different herbs have been used to mask the stink of mouth bacteria.

In one medical textbook from medieval Italy, a doctor advised people to grind up cinnamon, clove, spikenard, mastic, frankincense, grain, wormwood, crab foot, date pits and olives, and then chew them. Those are some very powerful flavours, and probably did a good job of masking any unwanted mouth odours.

Surely the worst mouthwash was the one that ancient Roman poet Catullus said people in Spain and Portugal used: their own wee! Maybe he was spreading nasty rumours about foreign people, so it might be untrue. But urine does have lots of uses, including whitening dirty clothes, so it wouldn't be surprising if there was some truth to the story. In which case … EUUUUGH, GROSS!

LIGHT BULB

Have you ever had a power cut in your house that lasted more than a few hours? I have, and it's amazing how quickly my life falls apart! No power means no charging my phone (boo!), no computer (double boo!), no TV (yikes!), no microwave or cooker (oh no!), my food spoiling in the fridge-freezer (disaster!), no heating (brrr!) and – of course – no light bulbs, so I bang into stuff in the dark (ouch!). Light bulbs are great inventions, but they need electricity to work, so let's start with that part of the story...

ANCIENT ELECTRICITY?

The internet is full of videos saying ancient Egyptians had electricity inside their pyramids, or that people in ancient Iraq had a "Baghdad Battery", a large pot they claim generated electricity. Sadly – spoiler alert – neither of these "facts" are true. Sorry! The Baghdad Battery was most likely a pot for keeping writing scrolls in, that's all.

However, we do know the ancients were curious about *static* electricity, which is that tingly charge you get when you rub a balloon against your hair and it stands on end. The Greek mathematician Thales of Miletus, who lived roughly 2,600 years ago, didn't have a balloon (he was a serious maths nerd, not a party clown), but he noticed that when he rubbed an *amber* gemstone (made from fossilised tree sap), nearby fluff and feathers were strangely attracted to it. He couldn't figure out why. However, the ancient Greek word for amber was *ēlektron*, which meant "shining like the sun", due to amber's orangey colour. That's where our word *electricity* comes from.

ELECTRIC ANIMALS

Ancient people also discovered that natural electricity was present in certain fish and eels. A Roman doctor called Scribonius Largus (great name!) gave his patients a shock from a torpedo fish – a type of electric ray – which he claimed would cure their headaches, epilepsy and foot pain. Bizarrely, if they had serious bottom problems, the doctor would give them an electric zap on the backside. Ouch!

ELECTRO-EXPERIMENTALISTS

Electricity also fascinated early scientists in the very late 1700s. The famous Prussian explorer Alexander von Humboldt repeatedly electrocuted himself to see what happened to his muscles, eyes, skin, tummy and bottom. (DO NOT DO ANY OF THIS, IT IS EXTREMELY DANGEROUS!)

At the same time, an Italian researcher called Luigi Galvani became famous for zapping frogs with electricity to make their legs twitch, while Eusebio Valli chopped off some frog legs, wired them together, and turned them into an electric battery – showing that there was natural electricity in living things. Galvani's nephew, Giovanni Aldini, went even further by electrocuting a huge ox's head, making its eyes roll around and tongue stick out. Creepy!

Horrifically, Aldini got bored of doing that and started using dead humans instead. These gruesome experiments were performed in front of audiences, and the terrifying reports made their way to a clever young English girl named Mary Shelley. The horrible idea of a scientist making dead muscles move later inspired her, aged only eighteen, to write the famous horror story *Frankenstein*.

VOLTA THE BATTERY BOFFIN

While these experiments proved living creatures have bodily electricity (*bioelectricity*), experts didn't think electricity could be generated any other way. However, along came another Italian physicist called Alessandro Volta in 1799, with his *voltaic pile* battery. Imagine a stack of cookies piled up on top of each other, but the cookies are discs of zinc and copper drenched with salt water. Hey presto, electricity! It was a huge moment in science and meant that modern batteries would eventually become possible.

ELECTRIC EDISON

One of America's best (and busiest) inventors was Thomas Edison, and the light bulb was his invention. Well, mostly... People had been trying to make them since the early 1800s, by running electricity through a metal strip, called a filament, until it glowed white. The problem was, they glowed waaaaaay too brightly, or burned out quickly. Research was needed!

Edison's team tested 3,000 bulb designs, and did over 6,000 experiments on different filaments. In 1879, they settled on carbonised cotton thread, which burned soft, bright, and didn't fizzle out fast. Result! Meanwhile, a British inventor called Joseph Swan made his own carbon filament bulb. A furious Edison tried to sue him for idea theft, but, weirdly, they ended up joining forces! Another inventor to mention is Lewis Latimer, a young patent expert who worked for another of Edison's rivals (he had loads!), and who improved how the filament was made. Edison spotted his talent and hired him too!

But hang on, how was electricity getting into people's homes to power these bulbs? They weren't plugged into frog-leg batteries!

THE WAR OF THE CURRENTS

Edison was also the first person to build an electricity power plant, in New York in 1882, which could power thousands of lights. His system of delivering electricity to homes was called Direct Current (DC). It was very expensive to run, and required chunky copper wires and lots of power stations around a city. But Edison had an ingenious rival, Nikola Tesla, whose different technology was called Alternating Current (AC). It was cheaper and could send powerful electrical currents from far away. A clever businessman named George Westinghouse bought Tesla's research, and then challenged Edison's company to see who would control electrical lighting in the USA. It was called The War of the Currents!

Edison refused to lose. He told everyone that AC was dangerous, and organised for journalists to watch stray cats and dogs being killed with Westinghouse's system. He even invented a word, saying people who got an electric shock had been "Westinghoused"! Despite these nasty publicity tricks, Edison did lose. Westinghouse had the better technology. By 1893, AC electricity, not DC, was being used in homes. In your face, sneaky Mr Edison!

WET WEATHER GEAR

It's nearly time to leave for school, but you hear a distant rumble of thunder. Uh oh! Looks like today's going to be rather soggy... Maybe it's worth a rethink on the outfit. Let's have a look at the options!

Shoo!

THE RAINCOAT

If you're heading out into the rain, you want a waterproof coat, right? A thousand years ago, people in medieval Europe mostly wore woollen clothing in bad weather, because wool remains warm even when it gets soaked through. So, the medieval solution to getting wet was … er … just to get wet, as long as you didn't catch a nasty cold. However, since ancient times, people in Japan wore amazing coats called *mino*, made of thatched straw or grasses. When woven together, this made a chunky, natural hat and cape outfit to keep the rain, snow and cold out. Anyone wearing it probably looked a bit like a scarecrow, but, frankly, if it kept them warm and dry, who cares?

ANORAKS AND PARKAS

Two modern styles of hooded coat are parkas and anoraks. Both are inspired by traditional coats used by Indigenous peoples living in the freezing Arctic Circle. These coats are tight-fitting, have furry hoods and are mega toasty. They are also fairly waterproof thanks to being made from the skins of seals or caribou deer, and then being rubbed down with fish oil. *Parka* is the name traditionally used by the Kivallirmiut people in Nunavut (northern Canada), whereas the Indigenous Inuit people of Greenland prefer *annuraaq* (anorak). These coats are mostly the same design, but if you went shopping for one today you'd see modern anoraks have no buttons, and parkas do. We also use the word anorak to mean someone who is very nerdy about a subject, so I suppose me explaining this to you makes me an anorak anorak!

That's a PARKA!

No, it's an ANORAK!

49

MR MAC

Of course, we also have another word for a raincoat – a *mac*! This is named after the Scottish inventor and chemist Charles Macintosh, who invented a way of waterproofing coats in 1823. His clever technique was to stick a layer of dissolved rubber in between two layers of fabric. Unfortunately, his coats were stiff, melted in the hot summer and smelled absolutely disgusting. In fact, some amusing reports said passengers in cramped carriages would chuck people off if they were wearing a mac because the stench was so intense in an enclosed space!

In 1839, a new technique of *vulcanising* (heating) the rubber solved all these problems, meaning the coats became more popular. Macintosh's company is still going today.

I gave Napoleon the boot!

WELLY BOOTS

If you're going to be tramping through big puddles, you need wellies! That's what we call them in the UK, but to everyone else they're just rubber boots. We call them wellington boots after the famous Duke who defeated Napoleon Bonaparte at the huge Battle of Waterloo in 1815. Wellington was well known for wearing smart, tight-fitting riding boots that nearly reached his knees, and the fashion caught on because he was such a military hero, and everyone wanted to copy him.

However, his boots were actually made of soft leather. Wellies didn't become rubber until the mid-1850s, when vulcanisation (which also improved Charles Macintosh's stinky raincoats) made the material ideal for sturdy footwear that could splosh and splash through muddy puddles without getting your socks all damp. But the Duke never saw his famous rubber wellies, because he died in 1852.

UNDER MY UMBRELLA

Another clever gadget for keeping the rain off our heads is the humble umbrella. The idea goes back over 4,000 years to the ancient Egyptians and Babylonians, but they all lived in very hot countries and so used them as *parasols* to keep the sunshine off their kings' heads. It was possibly the Chinese who realised, maybe 2,000 years ago, that these parasols could also keep people dry. Their umbrellas were made of silk initially (which is very strong), and then after a few centuries they also started using paper. To stop it going all soggy and turning into mush, Chinese paper umbrellas were coated in oil and lacquer, which made them usable on both sunny days and rainy ones. They were also collapsible, so they could be folded down when not needed. Smart!

Left a bit ... perfect!

Who needs umbrellas when you've got taxis?

The Italians and French were the first modern Europeans to embrace the umbrella. In 1710, a French inventor called Jean Marius filed a patent (meaning he registered his invention) for a clever folding umbrella that shrank down into a hand-held size, just like those Chinese ones.

But when a chap called Jonas Hanway brought the umbrella to England in the 1700s, he was widely mocked for what people said was his cowardly, silly, Frenchy fashion. He was particularly hated by carriage drivers and sedan chair carriers, who yelled insults and chucked rubbish at him. Why were they so angry? Because when it rained they got loads of customers who wanted to dodge getting soaked! Hanway's umbrella meant people could stay dry as they walked, so didn't need a taxi.

Gradually the umbrella became a bit less unpopular and by the mid-1800s, they were very common indeed. There were even various guides to good manners explaining how best to borrow an umbrella without seeming rude. As for the design, it really hasn't changed much from Jean Marius' version of 1710, although there were some pretty funny patents in the 1800s that didn't take off – my fave was an umbrella stored inside a top hat!

18 SHOES

When I was your age, I had to wear boring, black brogues with boring, black laces to school. I was constantly scuffing the toes playing football. But when did shoes first become a thing? Great question! My expert answer is ... er ... DUNNO? Sorry! The problem is, natural materials rarely survive for thousands of years, because they rot easily. Some archaeologists think humans started wearing shoes around 40,000 years ago. Experts have studied prehistoric skeletons and found people's big toes were suddenly getting weaker at this time. Maybe comfy shoes absorbed the impact of running, so the bone didn't need to be as strong? Nice theory!

STONE AGE SHOES

The oldest shoes ever found are 10,500 years old – WOW! Archaeologists discovered them in Oregon's Fort Rock Cave (north-western USA), and realised they'd been worn by ancient Indigenous Americans whose descendants (the Klamath Tribes) still live on the same land today. These strong sandals were woven from twisted cords of sagebrush bark, a hardy plant which thrives in the Oregon High Desert.

Indigenous Americans belong to many nations, each with its own language, territory and traditions. But they have often shared similar footwear – including leather slippers made from deerskin. In some Algonquian languages these are called *makasin*, and that word was borrowed by the European colonists who arrived in the early 1600s. Today, you can buy a pair of comfortable moccasins in any British or French shoe shop, but sadly not the brilliantly ancient sagebrush sandals. Pity!

POINTY POULAINES

It's easy to think of shoes as being just sensible foot-protectors, there to save us from the perils of wet puddles, sharp gravel and the disgusting squelch of dog poo. But shoes can also signal who we are in society, and how much cash we have in our wallet.

A marvellously strange example of this are *poulaines*, or *crakows* (named after the place in Poland where they originated). In the 1400s, these became very popular with rich European noblemen. Poulaines were ordinary shoes, apart from the long, pointy front that stuck out five inches beyond the wearer's foot. To stop this pointy bit going all floppy, it was stuffed with fabric, hair, wool or rigid material. Even then, it must have been very hard to walk in them without looking like a stumbling clown. In the most extreme examples, men tied the pointy bit to their knees with silk or chains to stop the shoe tripping them up. These shoes were purely about showing off, and that made them offensive to some religious thinkers, so King Edward IV of England passed a law banning them.

GOING UP IN THE WORLD

If longer was better for rich men in the 1400s, rich women in Italy were instead going for taller. They wanted to show off how much money they had by wearing the longest, most beautiful frocks, and the best way to lengthen a frock was to be higher off the ground. In Venice, posh ladies wore platform shoes called *chopines*, which were so tall they sometimes needed a friend either side of them to help them walk! Yup, some chopines were half a metre tall, which is basically a pair of stilts.

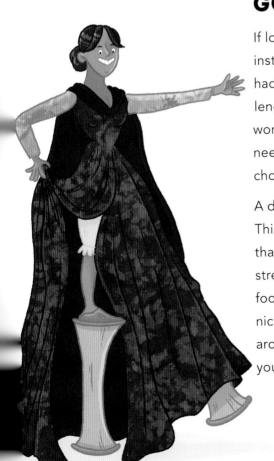

A different type of high shoe was also in use in medieval Europe. This was called a *patten* and it was a wooden sandal that people wore to walk in the muddy, poo-covered streets of big cities. Rather than being a shoe for your foot, this was a shoe for your shoe! You slid your nice footwear into the straps, and then stomped around with a few extra inches of height, to lift your cape or skirts out of the filth. Clever!

19

LETTER BOX

When you leave your house in the morning, do you ever arrive at the front door at the exact same moment the postie is stuffing mail through your letter box? Sometimes, as a joke, I like to stick my hand through suddenly and grab the envelopes straight out of their hand, as if there's a weird zombie living in my porch that eats pizza menus and electricity bills. The history of these letter boxes is relatively recent compared to a lot of other stuff in this book. So, let's find out why!

THE POSTMAN ALWAYS RINGS TWELVE TIMES

In London in the 1800s, posties didn't come once per day, but instead would go past the same house twelve times, meaning people with lots of friends (or enemies) could get a delivery every hour. In other big British cities it was more like six times per day, but that's still pretty good!

The constant door-knocking probably got a bit annoying, so a new invention arrived in Britain in the late 1840s. It was the humble letter box – a slit in the door, or a little outdoor box, which the postman could pop the letters into without disturbing the homeowner.

Not again!

KNOCK KNOCK, WHO'S THERE?

When the postie did need to deliver something face-to-face, they had to use a special knock. In the poshest of 1800s homes, rich people had many servants, including a butler or footman to answer the door. A guidebook written by an Italian visitor to London in 1837 said that "the manner of knocking at the door indicates the quality of the person who calls". Basically, your knocking style told the footman or butler who you were. Knocking too quietly was bad, but too loud was rude.

A single rap on the door was for the milkman, the man delivering coal, a servant or a beggar. The postman was meant to knock twice. Three knocks were for anyone who lived in the house but didn't have their own key, and four firm knocks followed by another four knocks were for announcing that a very important visitor was outside. If the visitor's servant knocked wrongly, they might be fired on the spot! Of course, if you heard more than eight knocks, that was probably a very confused woodpecker.

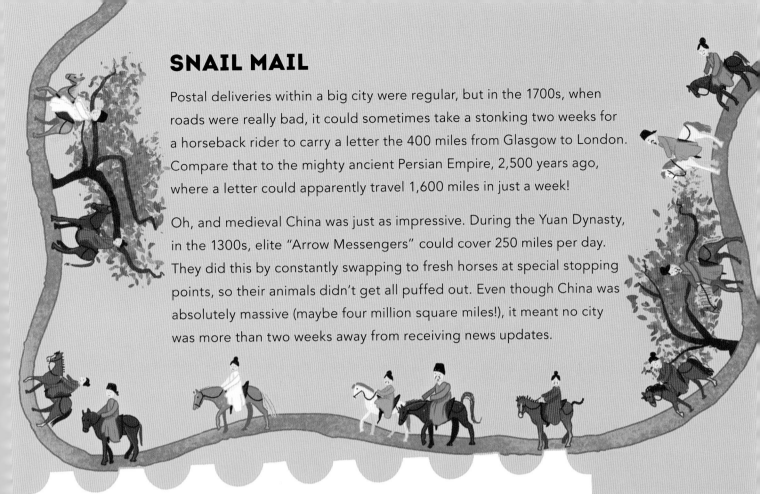

SNAIL MAIL

Postal deliveries within a big city were regular, but in the 1700s, when roads were really bad, it could sometimes take a stonking two weeks for a horseback rider to carry a letter the 400 miles from Glasgow to London. Compare that to the mighty ancient Persian Empire, 2,500 years ago, where a letter could apparently travel 1,600 miles in just a week!

Oh, and medieval China was just as impressive. During the Yuan Dynasty, in the 1300s, elite "Arrow Messengers" could cover 250 miles per day. They did this by constantly swapping to fresh horses at special stopping points, so their animals didn't get all puffed out. Even though China was absolutely massive (maybe four million square miles!), it meant no city was more than two weeks away from receiving news updates.

THE STAMP OF APPROVAL

The surprising thing about the British postal system 200 years ago is that the person sending a letter wasn't charged. Nope, it was the recipient who coughed up – I guess if you wanted to annoy someone, you could send them loads of letters! And it wasn't a standard fee either. It cost more if the letter travelled further, and also if it was written on multiple sheets of paper. To save money, people used a space-saving tactic called *cross-writing*, where they wrote from left-to-right, then from top-to-bottom. This meant there were sentences going down and across the page at the same time, like a very confusing crossword. To boast about how rich they were, wealthy people wrote with big handwriting, and left massive gaps in the margins. Show-offs!

All of this stopped in 1840, when Rowland Hill invented the Penny Black stamp. Sticking this on a letter of any size meant it could go anywhere in the country for a single penny. This invention was super important: it allowed millions of ordinary people to communicate more easily across the UK, and then across the world. It also allowed them to lick the back of the Queen's head, which is the only time you can do that without getting in a LOT of trouble!

CAR

You're running late, so your plan to cycle to school isn't going to work. OK, new plan! Grab a lift in the car and pop your bike in the boot, so you can ride home later. Of course, as you clamber into the comfy backseat, it's pretty obvious that cars are modern inventions – especially bits like the seatbelts, which have only been around since the 1960s. I say *modern* because lots of stuff in this book goes back thousands of years. But cars are older than you think, and the earliest ones were rather unusual...

THE FIRST CAR

What is a car, anyway? Well, *car* is an 800-year-old word, and originally meant a wheeled vehicle, like a wagon or a chariot. The most common car was a carriage, pulled by horses. And so, when cars with motors turned up in the late 1800s, people often called them "horseless carriages".

Even though people had been tinkering with the idea of motorised vehicles since the 1600s, historians say the first proper car was built in 1885 by the German inventor Karl Benz. It had three wheels, and no roof, doors or steering wheel! It was basically a padded bench plonked onto a large tricycle, with a small engine. To steer it, the driver had to use a *tiller* (a long rod with a handle), which is how people usually steer boats. To go left, you pulled it to the right, and to go right you pulled it to the left. This worked on smooth roads, but if the car hit a pothole, the tiller would often be jerked out of the driver's hand, making the car crash. Oops!

It didn't take long for designers to abandon the tricycle idea and add an extra wheel. And then, in 1894, they added a fifth – the steering wheel! This made crashing less of a problem, but only if you steered with both hands.

That's *wheely* embarrassing!

DRIVING ROUND THE BENZ

Karl Benz's local newspaper declared his car to be "useless, ridiculous, and indecent ... who is interested in such a contrivance so long as there are still horses for sale?" But people were interested, particularly when his wife, Bertha, and their two teenage children took it for a long drive, showing off how easy it was to use.

MAKING IT GO

Surprisingly, early cars weren't all petrol-driven. In the famous Paris-to-Rouen Race of 1894, the first competitive motorsport event, the winner was a steam-powered car driven by Jules-Albert, Count de Dion, followed by a petrol-driven car made by Peugeot. But the variety of engines on display included those powered by gravity, compressed air, gas, propellers, levers, liquid and – most surprising of all – electricity.

Yes, we assume electric cars are mega-modern feats of ingenious engineering, but battery power was already in use in the 1890s! The great American inventor Thomas Edison tried to mass-produce electric cars, which were particularly preferred by women because they were quiet and didn't make their clothes smell of petrol. Unfortunately, just as Edison was trying to perfect the battery design, oil became super cheap and easy to drill out of the ground, and Henry Ford designed his famous Ford Model T car. This was the first to be mass-produced

in factories using a production line, and it had a petrol-driven engine. The affordable, reliable Ford Model T became the most popular car in America, with 15 million sold between 1908 and 1927. The clever electric car never recovered from the competition. What a shame – just imagine how different the world might have been had Edison succeeded with his batteries.

DRIVING LAWS

Guess what the UK speed limit was until 1896? ONLY 4 miles per hour (mph)! In fact, it was a measly 2 mph in busy towns – that's belly-crawling speed! This law was originally created for steam-powered traction engines (tractors), and it also required a man to walk ahead of the tractor waving a red flag, to warn pedestrians of the chugging machine pootling up the road. Some early car drivers maybe had to follow these silly red flag rules too. In 1896 the speed limit increased to 14 mph (a decent sprinting pace if you're tired and old, like me). Cars now had honking horns to warn pedestrians, and the fella with the flag could go home to rest his aching feet.

ROMAN TRAFFIC JAMS

The idea of hiring a man to go ahead of your vehicle was actually something the ancient Romans had done 2,000 years ago. Very wealthy Romans would send their enslaved servant ahead to clear the roads, or hold up traffic like a set of traffic lights, so the rich person could avoid getting stuck in a boring jam. Rome, in particular, had a terrible traffic problem with lots of one-way roads, and both Julius Caesar and Emperor Claudius passed laws to ban carts during certain hours of the day. This was nice for pedestrians, but everyone transporting goods, building materials or food had to jostle in huge queues late at night or very early in the morning, and that is not a fun way to start or finish your day.

PENCIL CASE

Phew! You dodged the traffic and arrived at school just in time. But you'd better check you've got everything for your first lesson, so let's have a rummage in your pencil case, and see how old your stationery supplies really are!

DIGGING UP THE PENCIL

The humble pencil was invented in the mid-1500s. At some point, people in Cumberland (in north-west England) noticed a layer of weird, black, soft rock lurking under a tree that had been ripped up by a storm. We now call it *graphite*; it's a type of crystallised carbon that is flaky, soft and slippery.

People initially called it *black lead*, or *plumbago*, and the farmers in Cumberland first used it to mark their sheep, to stop them being stolen. But it was soon being used to scribble on other stuff that didn't say "Baa!". Artists used it to sketch things. In fact, pencil comes from an old word for a thin paintbrush. To prevent the black stains getting all over their fingertips, they wrapped the graphite in twigs, leaves, string or paper.

Need a pencil? We've got millions!

In the 1700s, carpenters figured out how to encase the graphite in wood, so it now looked like a proper pencil. Other places (France, Germany and the USA) were starting to make their own pencils by mixing graphite with clay, but the traditional Cumberland pencils were still the original and best. Sadly, the Cumberland mine ran out of graphite in the late 1800s, and an American called Joseph Dixon became the leading pencil-maker. By the 1910s there were 750 million pencils being made every year. (Wow! You wouldn't have wanted the job of counting them…) You could even buy them from special vending machines in the street – useful if your pencil snapped.

ERASING YOUR MISTAKES

If you make a blunder, it's no fun having to scrunch up your work and start again. In the 1950s, a clever American secretary called Bette Nesmith Graham had to type extremely quickly on the electric typewriter, and grew frustrated at making mistakes. So she invented a white correction fluid to paint over errors. For years it was just her cute little office trick, but when her friends kept asking to borrow it, she realised this was a great idea. She started her own company called Liquid Paper in 1956. Smart move, Bette!

Of course, if you make a mistake with a pencil, you can easily erase it with a rubber eraser. We owe this handy life hack to the English scientist Joseph Priestley, back in 1770. He also invented the word *rubber*, because he rubbed it against paper, but the plant it came from was actually called *caoutchouc*. Natural rubber was a bit flaky, though. Luckily, Charles Goodyear invented his "vulcanising" process in 1839 (remember the wellies and macs?). This made it strong and squidgy. In 1858, the first pencil with a rubber on the top was sold, and they're still useful today.

HOW LONG IS A METRE? 7 YEARS!

Rulers are for drawing straight lines or for measuring distance. It's the second one of those that I find very interesting, because who decided how long a *centimetre* is? Who declared what an *inch* was? Or a *metre*? Actually, that one I can answer.

In 1792 (during the French Revolution, when clever thinkers explored new ideas), big-brained scientists in France decided that a metre was "one 10-millionth" of the distance between the North Pole and the Equator (the band around the middle of the Earth). To measure this, two astronomers were sent off in different directions – one to Barcelona in Spain and one to Dunkirk in France. These two places were 1,000 km apart and aligned, one above the other, on the map, and that helped the maths boffins figure out how far away the North Pole was. Unfortunately, the two men kept being arrested for spying, as they were carrying suspicious surveying equipment – their mission was only meant to take a year, but it took seven long years to report back to Paris! The metre was finally invented in 1799, and a metal bar of that exact length was made so that scientists could use it as the standard unit of measurement.

I'm a scientist, not a SPY-entist!

HUMAN RULER

The ancients used the human body to measure length. Around 5,500 years ago, Egyptians used a *cubit*, which was the distance from a man's elbow to the top of his middle finger. The Greeks used a man's foot, and the Romans split a foot into 12 *uncia* (where we get the word *inches*). So, your 30-centimetre ruler is basically just the shoe size of a random bloke from 2,000 years ago.

How big?

This big!

University of Oslo 1940

PAPERCLIPS WITH PEOPLE POWER

The paperclips you and I know, with the lovely double loop of metal, are called Gem paperclips and were invented in America in the 1890s. There was an earlier, less good version invented in 1867. Oh, and a third type was invented in 1901 by a Norwegian man called Johan Vaaler, but it wasn't successful. And yet in Norway he became famous for inventing the Gem paperclip. Hang on, what?!

Well, in 1940 Norway was invaded by German troops loyal to the evil Nazi leader Adolf Hitler. The Nazis rounded up Jewish people, communists, disabled people, gay people, Romani and Sinti people, and many others, and they murdered them or sent them to horrific concentration camps. This also happened in Germany and other Nazi-controlled countries, such as France (my French great-grandfather and great-aunt were victims of this cruelty). In Norway, everyone else was told to start behaving like Nazis.

However, very brave students at the University of Oslo refused. To silently signal their resistance, they wore Gem paperclips as jewellery, to symbolise that proud Norwegians would hold together as one united people, just like a paperclip holds pages together. What an amazing idea! After the war, people got a bit confused and thought they had worn the paperclip because the Norwegian Johan Vaaler had invented this kind of paperclip – so he became associated with the paperclip he hadn't even invented. There's even a massive statue of a paperclip dedicated to him, but it's the wrong one! It's the thought that counts...

22 PAPER

I do all my writing electronically. (I certainly wouldn't want to write this book by hand – I'd get terrible cramp!) But, paper is still extremely common. It's used for books, newspapers, magazines, flyers, art – and I bet you use it for your schoolwork. But writing is much older than paper, so what did people in the past use instead?

CLAY TABLETS

Rather than being one great idea that spread around the world, writing was invented at least four different times (in Mesopotamia, Egypt, China and Central America). The first inventors were the Sumerians of Mesopotamia (modern Iraq), 5,200 years ago. Their writing was called *cuneiform* and it didn't use an alphabet. Instead, the symbols represented things people bought, and it replaced the older system where, if you'd bought a cow, you'd be given a cow-shaped token. Initially writing was just for accountancy – BORING! But after 700 years, it got more complex and could spell names and places, meaning people could write amazing stories about gods, monsters and heroic kings.

Cuneiform wasn't written on paper. A wedge-shaped *stylus* (reed pen) was pushed into a rectangular tablet of soft clay, which was then baked in the oven. Archaeologists have found tens of thousands of clay tablets from over 4,000 years ago that have loads of little dents in them. They look like chewed dog biscuits, but they're important ancient documents!

FROM PAPYRUS TO EARLY PAPER

Very soon after the Sumerians, the ancient Egyptians invented a writing system called *hieroglyphs*. As well as scribbling on the walls of tombs, they also wrote on *papyrus*. This was a plant that grew near the River Nile. They cut the stems into strips and smushed them together in a criss-cross pattern to make a *latticed* page, which they could write on in black and red inks.

We get our word *paper* from papyrus, but paper is different. It was invented in China over 2,000 years ago, but the most famous paper pioneer came later. He was called Cai Lun and in 105 he made paper by smushing together stuff like rags, fishing nets and plant fibres. Later paper-makers used cotton and linen fibres. Paper spread into the Middle East in the 700s, but took another 700 years to be widely used in Europe!

WROTE ON A GOAT

Paper wasn't popular in medieval Europe because people used *parchment* and *vellum*. Can you guess what these were made of? The answer is … dead animals! Yup, parchment was the cheaper version, made from the stretched-out skins of sheep and goats, whereas soft, pricey, high-quality vellum was made from baby cows. As a medieval history student, I studied books from 800 years ago where I could sometimes see the stretchmarks from the sheep's shoulders in the page!

The skins would obviously have been yucky and covered in blood, so they had to be soaked in water for a day, and then a caustic mineral called lime was added to remove the hair, which took over a week. The skins were then stretched on a frame, treated with various powders to absorb the grease – so the ink didn't run – and rubbed with things like flour, eggs and lime to lighten their colour.

HOW PAPER CONQUERED THE WORLD

So, how did paper replace parchment in Europe? It was thanks to the German inventor Johannes Gutenberg, whose printing press, invented in the 1450s, allowed for mass printing by using movable typeface. Books became cheaper and quicker to make, and paper was cheaper and easier to use than animal skins.

However, this soon caused paper shortages, which forced inventors to explore new ways to make it. People realised they could use wood, either by pulping it with machines or bleaching it with strong chemicals. It was then treated with animal glue or vegetable fats to stop the ink from running down the page, or blotting. This process is called *sizing*.

Annoyingly, this all had to be done by hand, one sheet at a time (imagine how long that took!). But, in 1807, England's Fourdrinier brothers, Sealy and Henry, made a machine that produced a huge, continuous roll of paper. In 1809, the Englishman John Dickinson cleverly added a rotating cylinder and, suddenly, paper could be cheaply mass-produced, meaning you can read this book!

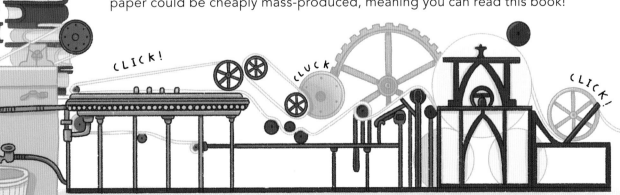

23 THE BOOK

Right now, in this very moment, you are enjoying a marvellous piece of technology. It has a front cover and a back, a spine down the middle, pages that are printed on both sides, and you can fold it in half. What is it? Yes, it's a ... *codex*! Hang on, no, that's not right – I meant *book*. Or did I? Hmm, how confusing! Let's start at the beginning...

FROM SCROLL TO CODEX

Before the book existed, first there were *scrolls*. We know ancient Egyptians wrote on papyrus, but when they scribbled long documents, they didn't turn their pages. No, they glued pages together, end-to-end, and then rolled them up. Think of it like a massive roll of toilet paper, with text on the inside. To make it easier to read, wooden handles (a bit like rolling pins) were added at each end, so a person could hold the top handle in their right hand and the bottom handle in their left.

Scrolls were used for centuries by ancient Egyptians, Jews, Greeks, Romans, Chinese and many others. But nearly 2,000 years ago, very early Christians started using a brand-new technology called the *codex*. It was basically a book, except the pages weren't yet made of paper. It was super useful for preaching Christianity, because you could easily flip to any Bible quote just by turning the pages, whereas scrolling up and down was way more of a faff!

GUTEN TAG, GUTENBERG!

In medieval Europe, books (known as *manuscripts*) were handwritten, usually by tired, squinting monks suffering with cramp. I'm not joking: on one manuscript a scribe wrote "Oh, my hand!" in the margins, while another complained: "Writing is excessive drudgery. It crooks your back, it dims your sight, it twists your stomach and sides." Poor chap!

This was the book-making process, until along came history's most famous printer, a German known as Johannes Gutenberg – remember him? (His real name was Johannes Gensfleisch, which vaguely translates to Johnny Gooseflesh!) Back in the 1450s, Gutenberg revolutionised the world by inventing the mechanical printing press. Using his converted wine press, books could now be cheaply mass-printed.

His key invention was movable type. Gutenberg arranged metal letters in a frame, coated them in ink, squished them against paper with the wine press, and could make many copies of each page before rearranging the letters to spell out the words for the next page, and so on. Images could also be copied thanks to three different techniques: woodblock printing, etching with acid and engraving.

Gutenberg's simple process caused an explosion in book-making, which allowed new ideas to spread faster and further. But – and it's a VERY BIG BUT – he wasn't actually the first person to invent printing. Nope, he may be the famous one, but the Chinese and Koreans got there first!

ASIANS DID IT FIRST

Woodblock printing is when you carve a design into wood, smear it in ink, then smush it onto a surface, so the inky outline transfers across. Chinese artists first did this 1,500 years ago, to print patterns on fabric. Around 1,200 years ago, it was used to make books too. It was a smart but slow process. Once carved, you could print many copies, but carving each page took aaages! For example, a huge collection of Buddhist writing, called the *Tripitaka*, used 81,258 individual woodblocks – that's a lot of trees and even more patience!

1,000 years ago, Chinese printers invented movable type using fragile clay blocks, but it didn't work too well. But 200 years later, a Korean politician named Choe Yun-ui switched to stronger metal instead – much better! By putting them in a frame, he could print entire pages in one go, then swap out the characters to write something different. Ingenious!

So, why doesn't Choe Yun-ui get all the credit? Alas, Korea was being invaded at the time, so it was hard for ideas to spread, and books were too expensive for most people. Many important nobles preferred traditional woodblocks, saying they were prettier. Another reason was that medieval Korean used the Chinese writing system, with its thousands of different symbols (called *logograms*) to represent words, sounds or grammatical instructions. Today the average Chinese speaker uses 8,000 characters – that's a lot of symbols to carve! Compare that to Johnny Gooseflesh (sorry, Gutenberg!) who only needed to rearrange 24 characters to spell every word in the German language. Perhaps this is why movable type printing didn't initially catch on in East Asia?

However, in the mid-1400s, along came a new printing pioneer: King Sejong of Korea. He was a big fan of printing. More crucially, he wanted ordinary people to learn how to read and write. So, he invented a new alphabet called *Hangul*, based on the spoken language Koreans used, not the written. Hangul originally had only 28 characters – much easier for printing. King Sejong and Gutenberg lived at the same time, and did similar things, but in different parts of the world. Cool, right?

CALCULATOR  24

What's 93 multiplied by 17? Tricky, isn't it? It takes me a minute to figure this out in my head, and, even then, I have to check my calculations. Maths is a fascinating and magical subject, but it's easy to make mistakes. The first electronic pocket calculator wasn't sold until 1972. Before then, people often did their sums by extracting the numbers out of their brains and plonking them onto something physical they could look at.

KEEPING TALLY

We can't be sure – they didn't leave us a note on the fridge to explain their thinking – but Stone Age people were probably doing maths over 40,000 years ago. Archaeologists have found animal bones inscribed with notches that seem to show complex multiplication. Researchers call these *tally-sticks*. They were used to remind people of complicated things (or in medieval business deals, the stick was split in half between buyer and seller, so both people had a receipt). The so-called Ishango Bone, discovered in Central Africa, dates to 20,000 years ago and has two rows of markings which each add up to 60. Was it a calendar for tracking the moon? Maybe!

Maths became really important 5,000 years ago, when tax collectors in Bronze Age empires needed to figure out who owed what to whom. The clever ancient Babylonians had a counting system based on the number 60 – just like the tally-stick from 20,000 years ago – where the number position mattered. Actually, we still do the same! The number 7,245 makes sense to us thanks to positional columns. The **7** represents thousands, the **2** covers the hundreds, the **4** is the tens, and the **5** is the ones. 7,245 = seven thousand, two hundred and forty-five. It's pretty amazing we're still doing this thousands of years later, isn't it?

When are you free?

Let me check my calendar.

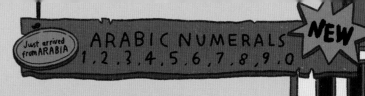

NAMING NUMERALS

You may know ancient Romans used their own numerals: I = 1, II = 2, III =3, IV=4, V = 5, X = 10, and C = 100. We don't use these, do we? No, we use 1, 2, 3, 4, 5, 6, 7, 8, 9 and 0. These are called Arabic numerals. They were actually invented by brainy ancient Indians, perhaps 1,500 years ago, and then they spread to the Middle East in early medieval times. This was a time of great scientific learning for Arab and Persian scholars, and their own exciting ideas were added to Indian ones, which then reached Europe. Because some Europeans didn't know the new number system had come from India, they mistakenly labelled them *Arabic* numerals. Oops, sorry, India!

MEDIEVAL MATHS MACHINES

In the medieval times, when an English king spent loads of dosh on fancy hats or foreign wars, his chief tax minister had to tot up the receipts and figure out how much to raise taxes to pay for it. They worked this out on a wooden counting board with lots of black and white squares, called an *exchequer*. This is why the UK's government minister in charge of the economy is called the Chancellor of the Exchequer, even though it's a totally ridiculous name.

Counting boards go back 4,500 years to the Bronze Age, but another counting gadget was the *abacus* (or *suanpan* in Chinese). These were used at least 2,000 years ago by various ancient societies, and were wooden frames surrounding metal rods on which you could slide beads up and down. The abacus had several rows of beads: the first row represented singles (1–9), the next row was tens (10, 20, 30, 40, 50), then hundreds, then thousands, etc. This made it easy to do big sums in your head, and it was easy to carry too. Also, the threaded beads didn't roll all over the floor if you accidentally dropped it – perfect for clumsy people!

COUNTING BOARDS

Before the abacus, a similar idea was widely used in the ancient world: a counting board. Lots of lines were drawn on a large wooden tablet or marble slab, to represent different number values. Pebbles were then put in the right place to help calculate large numbers. In fact, the Roman word for a pebble was *calculus*, which is where we get our word *calculator* (though if you smash one open you won't find any pebbles inside, obviously).

COUNTERS AND COMPUTERS

All these devices *helped* people count stuff, but they couldn't do sums for them! Actual calculators, which used cogs and wheels to crunch big sums for confused number numpties like me, arrived in the 1600s. However, they were expensive and rare. The first was a metal box called the *Pascaline*, named after its brilliant French creator Blaise Pascal. Then came the *Leibniz wheel*, invented by the brilliant German thinker Gottfried Leibniz.

In the 1820s, a brilliant British boffin called Charles Babbage designed a phenomenally complicated adding machine called a Difference Engine. He couldn't finish building it, so he then designed the even more complicated, steam-powered Analytical Engine, which was basically the first computer. He didn't finish that either! Babbage's friend, the young mathematician Ada Lovelace, wrote a translation and commentary on his invention, including a chart of her own calculations. For this, she is often called history's first computer programmer. Some historians disagree! They say it wasn't a proper programme, and Babbage had written his own anyway. But Ada is still mega cool because she was the first person to realise that a machine would one day be able to help make art and music. Ada is celebrated as the great visionary of modern computing – though she didn't predict playing a video game where you're a blue hedgehog who collects gold rings, did she?! Never mind, I'll let her off…

25 GLOBE

Is there a globe in your classroom? You know, a model of the Earth you can spin on its axis, perhaps to hunt for exciting places to visit when you're older? Or maybe you have a world map on the wall instead? Well, let me tell you a little secret: your globe is geographically correct, but your map is probably wrong! Let's find out why...

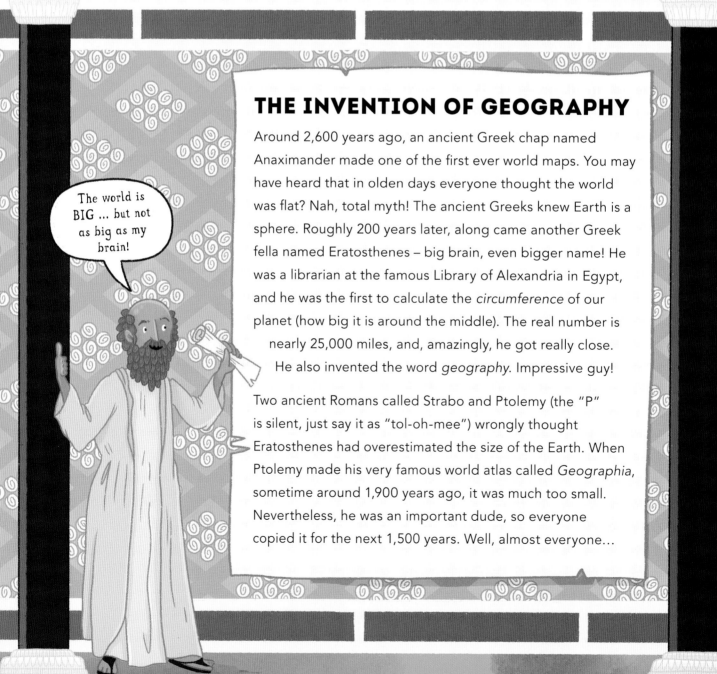

The world is BIG ... but not as big as my brain!

THE INVENTION OF GEOGRAPHY

Around 2,600 years ago, an ancient Greek chap named Anaximander made one of the first ever world maps. You may have heard that in olden days everyone thought the world was flat? Nah, total myth! The ancient Greeks knew Earth is a sphere. Roughly 200 years later, along came another Greek fella named Eratosthenes – big brain, even bigger name! He was a librarian at the famous Library of Alexandria in Egypt, and he was the first to calculate the *circumference* of our planet (how big it is around the middle). The real number is nearly 25,000 miles, and, amazingly, he got really close. He also invented the word *geography*. Impressive guy!

Two ancient Romans called Strabo and Ptolemy (the "P" is silent, just say it as "tol-oh-mee") wrongly thought Eratosthenes had overestimated the size of the Earth. When Ptolemy made his very famous world atlas called *Geographia*, sometime around 1,900 years ago, it was much too small. Nevertheless, he was an important dude, so everyone copied it for the next 1,500 years. Well, almost everyone...

MEDIEVAL MAPS

Medieval Arab scholars, such as Abu Rayhan al-Biruni and Muhammad al-Idrisi, made their own maps. Al-Idrisi's *Tabula Rogeriana* took him many years to make, and it was based on lots of interviews with sailors. It doesn't show most of Africa, and the Americas and Australia weren't yet known to such mapmakers, but it's really impressive on the European and Asian details. That said, if you were to look at it now, you'd be totally baffled – al-Idrisi put south at the top and north at the bottom, so it looks upside down to us.

Meanwhile, East Asian mapmakers (the fancy word is *cartographers*) focused more on China's trading neighbours – Africa, Arabia, India, South-East Asia, Japan, Korea and China itself. Perhaps the most famous survey of these regions is the *Kangnido* map, made in 1402 by two Koreans called Kwon Kun and Yi Hoe.

Now it's the right way up!

If you say so...

West Africa's miles away! Maybe I'll just say I went there...

GREG'S GREATEST

EARLY GLOBES

Perhaps the earliest globe was made in ancient Greece by Crates of Mallus. But the oldest surviving globe was the bright idea of German cloth seller Martin Behaim. In 1491–3, he convinced Nuremberg city council to hire craftsmen to cover a clay ball with fabric strips, then paint maps on them. This globe was nicknamed Erdapfel (Earth Apple) because it looks like a piece of tasty fruit. For centuries people claimed Behaim was a great navigator who'd charted West Africa's coastline. But his globe gets that bit totally wrong, so some historians think he just pretended he'd gone that far!

MODERN MERCATOR MAP MISTAKES!

Oh, and speaking of inaccurate maps… In 1492, the Italian explorer Christopher Columbus accidentally blundered into the Americas while seeking a speedier route to India's spices. He got confused (he hoped Cuba was Japan!), but others soon realised a new land had been discovered (new to Europeans, not to the Indigenous peoples who had lived there for thousands of years, obviously!).

So, did Columbus get to have this land named after him? Nope! In 1507, a mapmaker called Martin Waldseemüller gave that honour to another Italian explorer called Amerigo Vespucci, whose first name was tweaked to "America". The name stuck. In 1569, it showed up on a famous new map by Gerardus Mercator, whose design is still used today. Mercator drew his world map as a flat rectangle, but he'd actually flattened our ball-shaped planet into a curved cylinder with no top or bottom. Imagine peeling an orange then curling the skin into a hollow tube. This allowed navigators to plot easy straight-line routes, but it's terrible for showing what land actually looks like!

You see, Mercator maps distort and enlarge the places furthest from the middle equator, meaning Antarctica, Greenland and Canada are shown to be inaccurately huge. Mercator maps make Greenland equal in size to Africa, but Africa is actually fourteen times larger!

People have been arguing about how to make a better, fairer map for years – but all the new suggestions have problems too. That's why it's probably best if you stick to your globe!

Hang on, this isn't right!

ORBIS TERRAE COMPENDIOSA DESCRIPTIO

CHOCOLATE

Ah, it's time for a snack and that's my cue for some chocolate! The delicious, sweet, creamy stuff I cram in my mouth is pretty different from chocolate's origins. Yes, chocolate comes from the *cacao* tree, which produces *cocoa* beans (notice the confusing difference in spelling?), but it's only been a solid, chompable food for the past couple of centuries. Before that, it was a bitter drink.

FOOD OF THE GODS

Cocoa-slurping goes back over 5,000 years to the Mayo-Chinchipe people of Ecuador (South America), and later it became super important to the Olmecs, Maya and Aztecs (in medieval Central America). The Maya often drank their cocoa hot, jiggling the liquid between two cups to give it a big frothy foam on top – a bit like a cappuccino. Aztecs mostly drank it cold, mixing it with exciting flavours like honey, chilli, vanilla and special flower petals, and also adding maize (sweetcorn) to make a sort of bitter-tasting Coco Pops cereal, minus the milk.

The cacao tree has the scientific name *Theobroma cacao*, meaning "food of the gods" in ancient Greek. This is rather fitting, because medieval Maya art showed their gods helping the cocoa beans to grow by stabbing their ears with a sharp knife and bleeding all over the plant – not very hygienic! And when Aztecs sacrificed someone to their gods, they honoured their victim with a farewell drink of chocolate mixed with the blood of previous victims. Wowsers!

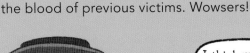

I think we've got too much froth!

73

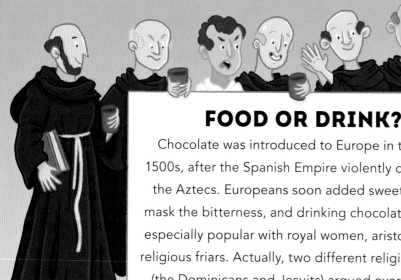

I declare, it's a DRINK!

FOOD OR DRINK?

Chocolate was introduced to Europe in the mid-1500s, after the Spanish Empire violently conquered the Aztecs. Europeans soon added sweeteners to mask the bitterness, and drinking chocolate became especially popular with royal women, aristocrats and religious friars. Actually, two different religious orders (the Dominicans and Jesuits) argued over whether chocolate was a food or a drink, because on holy days they weren't allowed to eat food, and they wanted to enjoy chocolate all the time! Luckily, the Pope decided it was a drink, not a food, so everyone could carry on guzzling choccie, even on holy days – hooray!

THE CHOCOLATE BAR

You might be thinking, "Hang on! These days chocolate is both a food AND a drink; when did it become chompable?" The answer to that is in the 1800s, when Britain became home to super-successful chocolate companies – like Cadbury, Rowntree's and Fry's – that helped make chocolate available to ordinary people.

They invested in big factories and new manufacturing techniques, such as the cocoa press (to squish out the cocoa butter) and the conching machine (to make the chocolate extra smooth). This led to the invention of my fave thing – chocolate bars. Unfortunately, in the early 1800s these were made of bitter dark chocolate (bleurgh!), but sweeter milk chocolate (yum!) was invented in the 1870s when Nestlé milk powder, meant for feeding newborn babies, was added to chocolate by a Swiss fella called Daniel Peter.

CACAO

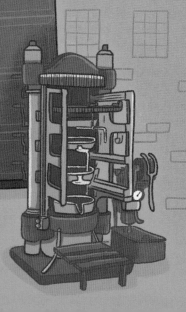

THE DARK HISTORY OF DARK CHOCOLATE

Sadly, chocolate also has a painful history. In the 1500s, Spain and Portugal colonised the Americas, and forced the Indigenous peoples (including the Aztecs) to keep growing cacao. But millions of these people soon died from a terrible disease. To replace them, the Spanish and Portuguese conquerors began a horrific system called the Transatlantic Slave Trade, and other European empires joined in. Millions of African people were enslaved and transported across the ocean in deadly, cramped ships. If they survived, they were brutally worked to death on sugar, cacao and cotton plantations in the Americas and Caribbean. Meanwhile, Europeans enjoyed chocolate and sugar as delicious luxuries.

Slavery made countries like Britain, France and the Netherlands very rich. Gradually, governments banned slavery for being cruel, but not everywhere at once. The British Empire outlawed it in 1833, but let it continue in India and Sri Lanka until 1843. Slavery carried on in secret in many places. In fact, in 1908 Cadbury was shamed for buying its cocoa from the Portuguese "Chocolate Islands" (near West Africa), where the workers were not free. Altogether, chocolate's tragic history is still very recent.

GREG'S GREATEST

I prescribe a bar a day.

CHOCOLATE MEDICINE

Here's how much I love chocolate – eating some, aged three, is my earliest memory! I'm not surprised it's lodged in my brain because this was an extra-sweet brand called Milky Bar, which had actually been invented in 1936 as a way of getting kids to take vitamin-boosting medicine. Back then it was called Nestrovit, but Milky Bar is more fun, I guess. It was perhaps good for your bones, but definitely not for your teeth!

27 BALL GAMES

If you had met me when I was thirteen, then you'd be a time traveller and that would be AMAZING! But also, you would have encountered a scruffy, muddy boy chasing a football like some overenthusiastic puppy. I would hurl myself around the hard concrete playground, launching my body into slide tackles or leaping to stop a goal. My knees were always bleeding! But my teenage football adventures were nowhere near as violent as medieval football. Count yourself lucky your playground games are nothing like it!

A GAME PLAYED ON FOOT, NOT WITH YOUR FOOT

The earliest mention of football dates back 1,200 years, but it was about 750 years ago that it got popular. "Folk" football was often played on special religious holidays in Britain, such as Shrovetide. Unlike the modern game of eleven players per team, medieval football was a teensy bit more chaotic. Teams were made up of whoever showed up, which might be an entire village, sometimes even 1,000 players.

Football was often played between rival villages and the goals were the gates of their respective churches. People probably carried, punched and kicked the ball – which was often made from a pig's bladder – and there was no referee, so no rules! Maybe you're wondering why it was called *football*, if people used their hands. Possibly because it was played "on foot", unlike posh people's sports which usually involved horse-riding. This was a game for ordinary people.

When you play football, the biggest risk is probably a twisted ankle, or getting the ball smashed in your face. But in medieval times everyone carried a knife on their belt for eating their lunch, so sadly there were lots of mid-game stabbing accidents! These violent ball games brought people together in big gangs, and that scared the powerful lords, who feared a peasant rebellion. This meant folk football was sometimes banned.

HERE COME THE RULES!

Despite starting as the ordinary people's game, by the 1800s football was most commonly played in very fancy English schools, like Eton and Harrow. But there were lots of different ways of playing, and it was only in 1863 that the English Football Association was created to make official rules for the sport. The most important, of course, was the "No Handball" rule. At last, football became all about using your feet … and definitely not a medieval dagger!

Foul! Use your feet!

No handball? It'll never catch on!

MESOAMERICAN BALL GAME

If you prefer basketball, volleyball or netball, let me introduce you to the ancient ball game played by the peoples of Mesoamerica (Mexico, Guatemala, Belize, Nicaragua, Honduras, El Salvador and Costa Rica). This was a game of skill and speed for two very small teams who competed on a long, narrow court with sloping stone sides. The game seems to date back 3,500 years, and is still played today.

The aim was to get the ball in the opposing team's endzone. A few courts have also been discovered that have a stone hoop, mounted high up on one of the walls. If the ball went through this hoop, that player instantly won, but this must have been really rare because it's super difficult to pull off that shot. Why? Well, the rubber ball was small but very heavy, and players weren't allowed to use their hands and feet. Instead, they mostly used their hips, and sometimes wore hip guards, kneepads, chest protection or thick girdles around their waists, to stop the ball bashing them too much. Even so, they would have been very bruised after a match.

Some people have claimed that the losing team was executed, because the courts were sometimes decorated with art showing people being beheaded. But most archaeologists think it was probably prisoners who were executed in front of the crowd – a bit different to the famous half-time spectacle at the Super Bowl!

PLAYGROUND GAMES

28

Maybe ball games aren't your thing? Or maybe you're under strict instructions not to tear holes in your school uniform again (I did this **A LOT!**). In which case, there are other things to entertain you in your breaktime. And these too might be older than they look...

GET YOUR SKATES ON

Remember the calamitous John-Joseph Merlin? He was wearing his newly invented roller skates when he smashed into a mirror in the 1760s. Skates didn't really take off (maybe his accident explains why!) until the 1820s, when a British chap called Robert John Tyers invented inline skates, which he called *Volito*. They looked like ice-skates, but with five small wheels instead of a metal blade. More importantly, the boots had brakes at the back and a stopper on the toe, so people didn't hurtle at high speed into any nearby glass. Sensible!

Four-wheeled roller skates, with two wheels on each side of the foot, were invented in 1863 by American James Plimpton. These were an improvement because the wheels could turn left and right, so people could easily change direction. He also set up skating rinks, where young people could hang out, have fun with their friends and flirt with attractive strangers. Skating became very popular in America and the UK in the 1870s, leading to newspapers calling it *rinkomania*! Weirdly, in 1917, a magazine even predicted that one day soldiers would move around the battlefield on roller skates. Obviously they'd forgotten about the mud. And the trenches. And the ... yeah, OK, I don't have to tell you how bad that idea was. Next!

Watch out!

ANCIENT GAMES

Some games seem to have been around for thousands of years. The ancient Romans and Greeks played with dice and with marbles (well, sort of – they may have used acorns or nuts), and they played a type of noughts-and-crosses with pebbles. They also had a variety of versions of tag, or chasing games. One Greek version, called *ostrakinda*, required two teams to stand on opposite sides of a line. A seashell or piece of painted pottery was chucked in the air, and, depending on which side it landed, one team became the chasers and another became the runners. There was also a version called the *copper fly*, where the chaser was blindfolded.

We also think the ancient Greeks and Romans probably played dodgeball. They definitely raced each other while rolling hoops on the floor, plus they did piggyback races with blindfolds on (don't do this near a pond or you'll get very wet!).

CLEVER CLIMBERS

In 1920, Sebastian Hinton, a lawyer from Chicago in the USA, invented the jungle gym climbing frame. But it wasn't his original idea – it had actually been the creation of his father, the famous mathematician Charles Howard Hinton. Charles had wanted to teach his kids some extremely complicated ideas about the shape of a theoretical, four-dimensional hypercube called a *tesseract* (this was a word he invented – you might recognise it from the Marvel superhero movies!).

To get his kids to open their brains to these bamboozling mathematical shapes, Charles built a big bamboo frame made of several interlocking cubes. He then named the poles things like X1, X2, X3 and Y1, Y2, Y3: he would shout the names out, and the kids were meant to scurry to those bits of the cube as fast as possible. Charles was hoping this was training his kids to understand the idea of the fourth dimension, but they were too busy having fun to learn any maths! When Sebastian grew up he wasn't a maths genius, but he remembered that he'd enjoyed the climbing frame, so he built a jungle gym to let kids explore their adventurous instincts!

I said X1 NOT Y3!

THE UPS AND DOWNS OF THE YO-YO

Yo-yo: it's such a fun word to say! When was it invented? We don't know! Some say it was in ancient China – but there is also one shown on a piece of beautiful ancient Greek pottery from 2,500 years ago. A similar toy, called a *diabolo*, was very popular in medieval China and then spread southwards to the islands known today as the Philippines. This diabolo had a much wider spinner, and was rolled around on a string connected by two sticks.

The yo-yo came back to Europe in the 1700s, where it was often known as a *bandalore*. It was a trendy plaything for very wealthy French nobles, young and old, and there's a famous painting from the 1780s of the young Prince of France looking adorably cute while holding one. But then political disaster struck! The French people rose up against the royals during the French Revolution in 1789, and most of these rich nobles were arrested and executed with a head-chopping machine called the guillotine. Those who managed to run away took their yo-yos with them, which is why these beautiful toys became known as either *emigrettes* (meaning "people who leave") or as *de Coblenz*, which was the name of a German city many of them fled to.

But, wait! We've heard several different names, but no explanation for why it's now called a yo-yo. Well, you'll hopefully remember that these toys were very popular in the Philippines. Yo-yo means "come, come!" in the Filipino language, because you jerk the string of a yo-yo to make the spinner come back to you. In 1898, the Philippines were seized by the USA and became an overseas territory, and that meant the toys were soon brought to America, where they kept their cheery name and became popular all over again.

Yeah, it's more of an up and down motion...

Oh...

WATER FOUNTAIN

29

Does your school have a water fountain? Obviously I mean a drinking fountain, not some massive ornamental sculpture of a gargling mermaid! Although, if your school does have that, you must go to a **VERY** impressive school. Anyway, when I was a child, we had to angle our head sideways at the fountain to catch the water, and sometimes it would squirt me in the face! But I'm not bitter about it... In fact, I love fountains because they have a rich and fascinating history.

DRAIN BRAINS

History's most impressive water-wranglers were the Indus civilisation (in what is now India and Pakistan). These Bronze Age brainboxes were masters of *hydro-engineering* (*hydro* means water in ancient Greek), and their biggest cities had over 700 wells, drainage channels, indoor plumbing, public baths and fountains. Basically, they made quite the splash! Even though they lived 4,000 years ago, the Indus people were so advanced, it took until the mid-1800s before Londoners could enjoy the same standard of water engineering. Amazing, right?!

AMAZING AQUEDUCTS

Aqueducts are pipes or watercourses that carry water from one place to another, and the absolute masters of this technology, 2,000 years ago, were the ancient Romans. Whereas previous civilisations preferred to run water through underground tunnels and channels, this bunch built massive, ten-metre-high aqueducts supported by stone arches, running over 50 miles in length! The city of Rome needed eleven of these aqueducts to deliver vast quantities of fresh water, and there were many more serving the other cities in the empire.

The marvellous thing about transporting water high off the ground is that, when it gets to the end of its journey, it can race downhill and build up a lot of pressure. This meant it didn't just trickle pathetically out of pipes, but could instead gush upwards into the air, producing an impressive spurting fountain. No pumps were needed – gravity did the hard work! The Romans were obsessed with water, and one of the best ways of showing off was to have a fountain in your garden. It was a sign that you were proper classy.

Woah! You must be rich!

FIGHT FOR FOUNTAIN FAIRNESS

Sadly, fountains have painful histories too. In the 1950s, in the southern states of the USA, racist rules called "Jim Crow laws" meant white people were considered racially superior to African-Americans. Black people had to go to their own schools, weren't welcome in shops and restaurants, had their own public toilets and, on the bus, they were forced to give up their seat if it was busy. Even children were *segregated* (kept apart) at drinking fountains.

The American hero Rosa Parks – who, in 1955, refused to stand up for a white person on a bus, and helped start a famous bus boycott protest – said that as a girl she had "wondered if 'white' water tasted different" from the water she was allowed to drink. Later on, as a protestor for racial equality, she escorted groups of Black teenagers to drink from the white fountains, to show that all people should be treated the same. In 1964, the Civil Rights Act made segregation illegal and fountains became available to everyone, no matter who they were.

FOUNTAINS FIT FOR A KING

King Louis XIV of France was perhaps Europe's most powerful ruler in his lifetime, and in the 1680s he demanded glorious fountains to decorate the palace gardens at Versailles. To make these work, his engineers spent seven years building an enormously complicated system called the Machine of Marly. It cost a fortune and involved fourteen water wheels (each twelve metres wide) that were turned by the current of the River Seine. They powered 200 water pumps, which pushed a million gallons of water uphill into two big reservoirs. The water then ran downhill, copying the Roman gravity technique, to give King Louis his impressive fountains. It was an astonishing mechanical marvel, but it was noisier than a heavy metal concert. King Louis' guests complained a lot – but he probably couldn't hear them, to be honest...

A MIGHTY MONGOL MACHINE

A smaller, but equally impressive, fountain was made in medieval Mongolia in East Asia. Back in the mid-1200s, a European traveller called William of Rubruck went on a very, very long journey to the court of the powerful Mongol emperor, Möngke Khan, and its capital Karakorum. Here William encountered a beautiful sculpture of a tall, silver tree, on top of which was an angel blowing a trumpet. At the base were four sculpted lions, and high in the branches were four serpents. But here is the fun bit – these eight terrifying beasts didn't devour passers-by. No, quite the opposite – they dispensed tasty drinks from their mouths! The lions provided fermented horse's milk, and the serpents provided honey mead, wine and rice wine.

Obviously, it was very wasteful to have the drinks constantly sloshing about, so the fountain was only used when Möngke Khan got thirsty. When he demanded a drink, a man would squeeze inside the tree trunk and blow into a bellows. This made the angel raise its trumpet and parp a loud sound, which alerted the other servants to fetch the drinks. They poured them into holes at the base of the tree, and the liquid was then sucked up and squirted out of the animals' mouths. What a palaver for a simple cup of wine!

Do you have any orange squash?

30

CLASSROOM CLOCK

Your lesson is dragging on a bit, and you wonder how long it is until you can go home. You take a sneaky glance at the clock, and see that it's only been four minutes since you last looked. What?! Time moves soooo slowly when you're bored! If only this next hour were a bit shorter, right? Well, centuries ago, it would have been...

HOW LONG IS AN HOUR?

The history of telling the time is strange. Until 1371 – when a clever Syrian Arab astronomer called Ibn al-Shatir invented an accurate *equal-hours* sundial – hours were longer in the summer and shorter in the winter. You might be thinking, "Surely an hour is always 60 minutes long?!" Well, yeah, now it is. But not back then.

We get our 24-hour day from the ancient Egyptians. Just like the Babylonians, they loved using the number 12 in their maths and said a day should have 12 hours (1 hour of dawn + 10 hours of light + 1 hour of dusk = 12). That left 12 hours of darkness. But summer is much sunnier than winter, isn't it?

So, though ancient Greek philosophers divided a day into 24 hours of 60 minutes each, ordinary people knew that hours were longer in the summer – about 75 minutes! – because 12 hours of daylight had to stretch to fill the 15.5 hours of summer sunlight! And in winter, daylight hours squeezed to 45 minutes instead. It's a real brain-melter, isn't it?

You're an hour late.

No, we're on summer time!

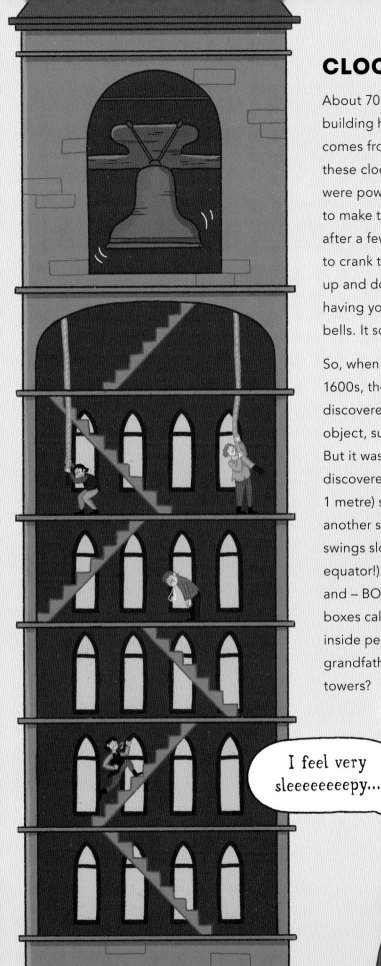

CLOCKS THAT GO BONG

About 700 years ago, important European cities were building huge mechanical clocks in bell towers (*clock* comes from the Latin word for bell, *clocca*). Unfortunately, these clocks were rubbish at keeping reliable time. They were powered by massive weights that pulled on ropes to make the complex clockwork tick back and forth, but, after a few hours, the ropes went slack and engineers had to crank the weight up to the top again. Imagine running up and down all those stairs, hauling massive weights, and having your eardrums bonged into oblivion by those loud bells. It sounds like a stressful job...

So, when did clocks become more accurate? In the early 1600s, the ingenious Italian astronomer Galileo Galilei discovered the *pendulum effect*. This is when a dangling object, such as a yo-yo, swings back and forth on its own. But it was the brainy Frenchman Marin Mersenne who discovered that a pendulum 39.1 inches long (almost 1 metre) swings for an exact second one way, then another second back the other (though a pendulum swings slower the closer you get towards the Earth's equator!). Pendulums made clocks more accurate, and – BONUS! – they could now fit in wooden boxes called *grandfather clocks*, which could go inside people's homes (but not inside people's grandfathers, obviously). Who needs bell towers?

I feel very sleeeeeeepy...

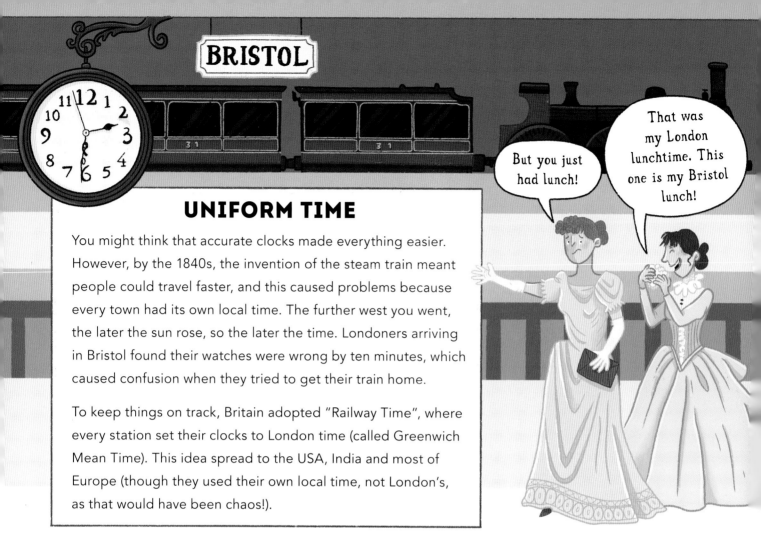

BRISTOL

But you just had lunch!

That was my London lunchtime. This one is my Bristol lunch!

UNIFORM TIME

You might think that accurate clocks made everything easier. However, by the 1840s, the invention of the steam train meant people could travel faster, and this caused problems because every town had its own local time. The further west you went, the later the sun rose, so the later the time. Londoners arriving in Bristol found their watches were wrong by ten minutes, which caused confusion when they tried to get their train home.

To keep things on track, Britain adopted "Railway Time", where every station set their clocks to London time (called Greenwich Mean Time). This idea spread to the USA, India and most of Europe (though they used their own local time, not London's, as that would have been chaos!).

GLOBAL TIME

Hey! You're meant to be in our time zone!

In the 1870s, a Canadian railway engineer called Sandford Fleming argued there should be 24 different time zones around the world, with the time changing one hour for every 15 degrees of *longitude* – that's when you move left (west) or right (east) on a globe.

In 1884, the world's biggest countries decided Greenwich Royal Observatory in London should be the starting point (or *prime meridian* in scientific speak), then you'd gain hours if you moved east, and lose hours if you went west. Huge countries like the USA needed several different time zones, because they cover way more than 15 degrees of longitude on a map.

However, it still got a bit awkward. Paris is only 2 degrees east of London, so both cities should share the same time zone. But Nazi Germany invaded France in World War Two, and forced them to use German time. After the war, the French didn't change it back. So, Paris is one hour ahead of London, even though they're really close!

SMARTPHONE

Of course, many of us don't use clocks to tell the time – I just use my smartphone. Yeah, it's the most amazing technology, with a camera, videos, songs, apps, games, texts, phone calls and even a torch, all in one little box. IT'S ACTUAL MAGIC! A simple smartphone is way more powerful than the computers that put humans on the Moon in 1969, and yet we just walk around with it, like wizards with wands in our pockets. But smartphones aren't the first technology to let us speak to people far away. Long before gadgets and microchips, there was good old flag-waving and fire signals!

LONG-DISTANCE CHAT

Imagine you're a Babylonian king ruling a mighty empire 4,000 years ago. How do you send emergency messages to faraway cities? There's no way a runner, or a horse, or even a carrier pigeon can travel hundreds of miles in a few minutes. The answer is with fire beacons. So, how did it work?

All you had to do was build watchtowers on a high point, every few miles. They needed to be close enough that they could see a burning beacon on the horizon, but far enough away that it wouldn't be quicker to just run over and say "hi!". In an emergency, anyone in that chain – from the king in his palace, to a soldier on duty – could raise the alarm by lighting their beacon. The next set of watchmen would see it, and ignite theirs, and then so on, until the message had spread over hundreds of miles. And that message was presumably, "UH OH! SEND HELP!"

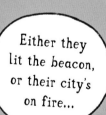

Either they lit the beacon, or their city's on fire...

You see, that's the thing with fire beacons – you have to agree on the message in advance, because they're either on or they're off, but you can't spell anything out. In 1588, when England was under attack from the Spanish Armada (an invasion fleet of warships), beacons were lit along the coastline to warn Queen Elizabeth I and her advisers. But the beacons couldn't say anything other than, "YIKES, VERY BIG INVASION!" They were quite literally fire alarms.

SPELL IT OUT

In ancient Greek times, about 2,200 years ago, a writer named Polybius worked on a messaging system that let people send text over long distances. He put the Greek alphabet on a grid, five boxes wide and five going down. If "A" was one along and one down, then the messenger would have to light one flaming torch to the left of a marker and one to the right. Or to spell "M", which was two along and three down, the messenger had to light two torches to the left of the marker and three to the right. In theory, Polybius was a genius, but we don't think his idea caught on. Sounds like it was a bit too fiddly.

SEND KELP? I think that might be a typo...

Lost again!

TELEGRAPH TOWERS

When you send a text to your friend, you are technically doing something called *telegraphy*. This is ancient Greek for faraway (*tele*) + writing (*graph*). The message travels through radio waves and then along cables that run around the world. Pretty impressive, right?

But before electronics were invented, there were other ways to send complex messages. In the late 1700s, France's Chappe brothers improved upon Polybius's idea by building tall telegraph towers that had a beam, called the *regulator*, which could be moved into four positions. There were also two flaps that could be moved into seven positions each. This meant there were 196 possible positions, which the Chappes matched to a special codebook.

Whereas Polybius had tried to write words letter by letter, which took blooming ages, the Chappes just told the people in the receiving tower to look up a word in the codebook. A simple message of "2, 45, 48" meant "the 48th word on page 45 of book 2". Clever, huh? With this cunning system, Revolutionary France was also able to speedily transmit the national lottery results around the country, which probably led to lots of people being grumpy that they hadn't won anything.

NEWS TRAVELS FAST

Outside of France, long-distance messaging really took off when it harnessed the whizztastic power of electricity. In Britain, the telegraph machine was invented by William Fothergill Cooke and Charles Wheatstone in 1837. They figured out a way to get electromagnets to push/pull in different directions, and so point at different letters. The message – or *telegram* – was converted into a signal and sent down chunky cables, and could travel much, much further and faster than a man on a horse. By 1858, a huge undersea cable was laid in the Atlantic Ocean to connect North America and Britain (it proved an embarrassing disaster when the cable soon stopped working, but they tried again a few years later with greater success).

The USA had its own telegraph machine, invented in 1838 by a painter called Samuel Morse, which became very popular around the world. Rather than using the alphabet, Morse instead created a coded language of beeps! Yes, noisy dots, dashes and spaces represented letters, and this became known as *Morse code*. Telegraph operators had to learn this language and then translate it onto paper for customers to read, and they could do 40–50 words per minute. That might not impress you now, but in the mid-1800s this was a jaw-droppingly amazing techno-revolution!

In fact, the arrival of telegrams was truly world-changing. People were used to waiting weeks for news from faraway places, and suddenly battles in the Crimean War, 2,000 miles from London, could be reported that afternoon! This was amazing, but also a bit intense. People complained the world was getting too fast; doctors even said a new imaginary disease called *Neurasthenia* (nicknamed *Americanitis* in the USA) was making people tired and headachey. The cause? The speed of modern life! There was just TOO MUCH INFO!

TELEPHONE

These days, mobile phones are so common, but I didn't get my first one until I was nineteen. It was very basic, could barely go on the internet and didn't even have a camera – but it was surprisingly strong (I accidentally ran it over with my dad's lawnmower, and it was fine!). Back then, being able to walk around and call people from anywhere was really new. But imagine how exciting it was when the phone was first invented, way back in the late 1800s...

GIMME A BELL

Here's a simple question: who invented the telephone? The official answer is the Scottish-American inventor Alexander Graham Bell, in 1876. But this is where things get tricky...

You see, before Bell, several others had experimented with sending sound through electrical wires, including the Frenchman Charles Bourseul, the German Johann Philipp Reis, the Italians Antonio Meucci and Innocenzo Manzetti, and then – most controversial of all – the American Elisha Gray, who submitted his telephone design at the patent office (where new inventions are legally registered) on the VERY SAME DAY as Alexander Graham Bell. What a coincidence!

As for Antonio Meucci, history was so nearly very different. A few years after Bell's success, Meucci's design was recognised as having got there first, but, sadly, he'd been too poor to afford the renewal fee on his patent. If he'd had just $10 spare, he might have become the most powerful man in the telecommunications biz! Poor old Meucci ... he was too poor to become rich.

HELLO!

According to legend, when Bell demonstrated his new-fangled gadget to Thomas Edison, the superstar American inventor, Edison was so startled he shouted "HULLO!". This was an 1800s exclamation of shock, the sort of thing you'd blurt out if you bumped into your teacher on holiday.

This story might be untrue, but Edison definitely suggested "Hello!" should be the official telephone greeting, as he assumed telephone lines would always be open, and there wouldn't be a ringing sound to start each call. He thought people needed a new word that they didn't say in normal office chat, so, if they heard it, they'd realise it was someone on the phone.

"Hello" became the official telephone greeting, and then spread to everyday usage. In fact, it's now one of the most popular words on the planet. But – fun fact alert! – Bell wanted the phone greeting to be "Ahoy!". Imagine saying "Ahoy!" every day … you'd feel like a pirate!

MIND YOUR MANNERS

New inventions can force people to figure out new ways of behaving. When the coronavirus pandemic struck in 2020, and people had to stay at home and do their school lessons or jobs online, they learned to politely take it in turns when chatting on a group video call, otherwise they'd produce a noisy and confusing cacophony. But it was even more confusing in the late 1800s, when new telephone technology was like nothing ever known before.

Some people were terrified that telephones would let strangers annoy them, or try to sell them stuff. The high-class types wondered if it was rude for a man to telephone a woman if he wasn't standing up, or wasn't wearing trousers – yes, even though she couldn't see him! People also feared they could catch disease down the phone line. It's funny to us, but the telephone was both exciting and scary to people who'd lived their lives without such amazing technology.

33 BICYCLE

You've finished school and it's stopped raining, so you hop on your bike and pedal home. When I was younger, back in the summer holidays my friends and I would race our bikes downhill through the woods, doing our best not to get flung off by knobbly tree roots sticking out of the ground. (Obviously, it's very, VERY important to wear a helmet.) Of course, our mountain bikes were strong, lightweight, and had twenty-one gears. If we'd tried it with bikes from the 1800s, we might have had some nasty accidents...

Where's your horse?

PASSENGER POWER

A bicycle has got two wheels, right? The clue's in the name: in Latin *bi* = two, and *cyclus* = circle. But the story of bicycles might start with a strange four-wheeled machine invented 600 years ago in northern Italy, by a chap named Giovanni Fontana. His idea was a cart – it looked more like a golf buggy than a bike – powered by ropes, looped around big gears, which were pulled by the passenger. It was a vehicle propelled by the user, not pulled by an animal, and this was a brilliantly revolutionary idea ... which was completely ignored by everyone. D'oh!

Roughly 275 years later in the 1690s, a French inventor called Jacques Ozanam came up with something similar, but his carriage carried two passengers – one to steer, and the other to power it by stepping up and down on moving treadles. With four wheels, it still wasn't a bike, but that sounds a bit like pedalling, right? In the 1700s, various people tried to build similar contraptions, but they never caught on either. Oh well.

BEWARE THE BONESHAKERS!

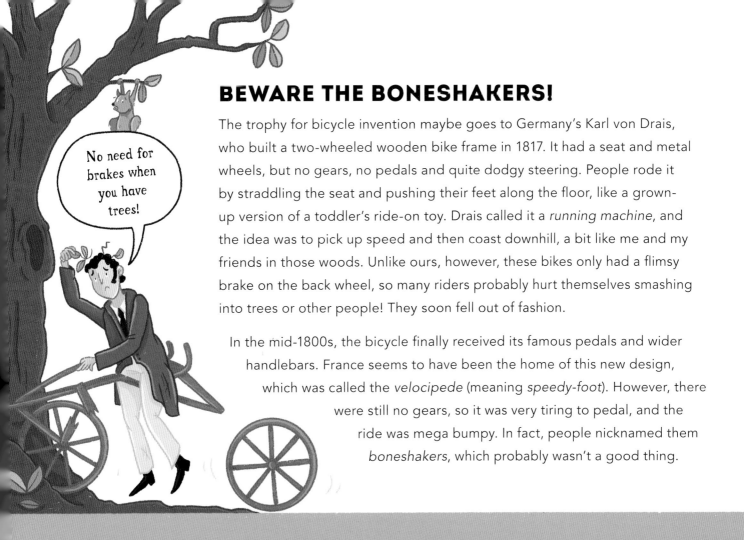

The trophy for bicycle invention maybe goes to Germany's Karl von Drais, who built a two-wheeled wooden bike frame in 1817. It had a seat and metal wheels, but no gears, no pedals and quite dodgy steering. People rode it by straddling the seat and pushing their feet along the floor, like a grown-up version of a toddler's ride-on toy. Drais called it a *running machine*, and the idea was to pick up speed and then coast downhill, a bit like me and my friends in those woods. Unlike ours, however, these bikes only had a flimsy brake on the back wheel, so many riders probably hurt themselves smashing into trees or other people! They soon fell out of fashion.

In the mid-1800s, the bicycle finally received its famous pedals and wider handlebars. France seems to have been the home of this new design, which was called the *velocipede* (meaning *speedy-foot*). However, there were still no gears, so it was very tiring to pedal, and the ride was mega bumpy. In fact, people nicknamed them *boneshakers*, which probably wasn't a good thing.

No need for brakes when you have trees!

A WHEELY STRANGE IDEA

Nobody wanted to rattle and bounce along the road, so the next big idea was to make bicycles comfy to ride. In 1869, one solution was to have a humungous wheel at the front, and a small one at the back. This meant you could go faster, and new wire spokes in the wheel absorbed some of the horrible boneshaking vibrations. However, clambering onto this very tall bike was no easy feat, and falling off was even more painful! Known as a *high-wheeler*, these metal bikes were famously renamed the *penny-farthing* in the UK, because the wheels looked like the large penny coin next to a small farthing coin.

High-wheelers stopped being popular in the 1880s, when the so-called *safety bicycle* – with its multiple gears, rubber tyres and lower height – was widely marketed. And many of the most enthusiastic cyclists on this new bike were women, which caused a bit of a hoo-ha…

Has anybody got a ladder?

93

BEWARE BICYCLE FACE!

The humble bicycle was super important to British women in Victorian times because it allowed them independence to travel on their own, without a chaperone to ensure they were behaving themselves. Unfortunately, ladies' skirts got caught in the wheel spokes, so they started wearing *rational cycling dress* (remember our previous chat about Amelia Bloomer?). Sensible, right? Well, this made lots of people absolutely furious. "LADIES IN TROUSERS?! IMMORAL AND WRONG!" they shouted.

Some medical experts tried to discourage women by saying bicycles would jiggle their insides (not true!), so they wouldn't be able to have babies (not true!), and that going downhill too fast would make their faces permanently contort into ugly expressions called "BICYCLE FACE!" (definitely not true!). People had been riding horses for thousands of years, but as soon as women wanted to go fast, lots of ridiculous excuses were made up to stop them. Luckily, it didn't work.

Urgh! Look what cycling did to her face!

GREG'S GREATEST

CYCLING ENTHUSIASTS

The country most famous for its love of bicycles is China, which has an estimated half a billion bikes! The first bikes arrived from Europe in the late 1800s, but they didn't get popular until the 1950s. By the 1970s, absolutely everyone had a bike, and rush hour traffic was almost entirely people pedalling to work! These days there are lots more cars, but bikes are still very popular.

POTATO CRISPS

34

You've made it home and all that cycling has left you feeling peckish, so it's time for an afternoon snack. I recommend a healthy bit of fruit, but you might prefer a packet of crisps (known as chips in the USA). These are very common potato snacks today, but did you know the humble spud has a really long and surprising history?

PERU'S POTATOES

If you look at a map of South America, you'll see the huge Andes mountain range running down the western side. The people living there 8,000 years ago, in what is now Peru and Bolivia, started farming a new type of wild plant: the potato, a remarkably adaptable crop that grows even in cold mountain regions.

Potatoes are brilliant. They are jam-packed with energy, starch and vitamins. And these ancient Andeans figured out how to freeze potatoes for long-term storage. They left them outside to freeze at night, then jumped on them to squash out the water, then froze them again, then dried them in the sun. Amazingly, these dried-out spuds (known as *chuño*) could be kept for over ten years without rotting, which was a lifesaving back-up if the maize (corn) harvest failed. All they had to do to make the chuño edible was add water – yup, even in the Stone Age, people had instant mash! Today, thousands of years later, chuño is still a big part of Peruvian cooking.

Stored for ten years and still delicious!

YUCK! I forgot to freeze mine!

35 SOFA

While you're enjoying your salty snack, you may as well make yourself comfy. Certainly, when you get as old as me, you will welcome a nice sit-down! You may even make a little sound, like "Aaaah, that's better!" when you plonk yourself down on the sofa. The word *sofa* comes from the Arabic *suffah*, meaning a place of shelter or comfort – but sitting hasn't always been about being comfy...

SITTING SEIZA

In Europe and North America, it's long been normal to sit on furniture – chairs, sofas, benches, stools, etc. But in East Asia, people have traditionally been more comfortable down on the floor, perhaps sitting on *tatami* mats made of straw and rushes. For centuries, the polite Japanese way of sitting has been called *seiza*. These days, there are different styles that are more relaxed or more appropriate to certain situations, such as the cross-legged *agura* style, or the *tatehiza* pose with one knee raised, which was used by samurai warriors. You might sit like that quite often.

The most important pose of seiza – used in very polite situations to show respect to others – is to sit on the knees with feet folded underneath, so your bottom is cupped by your ankles. You must have a very straight back and not fidget! Bending your joints like this is painful if you haven't done it your whole life, and it's tricky to do in tight trousers. Today, seiza is less common in Japan, except during formal tea ceremonies. But many people still like to sit on the floor.

POTATO CRISPS

You've made it home and all that cycling has left you feeling peckish, so it's time for an afternoon snack. I recommend a healthy bit of fruit, but you might prefer a packet of crisps (known as chips in the USA). These are very common potato snacks today, but did you know the humble spud has a really long and surprising history?

PERU'S POTATOES

If you look at a map of South America, you'll see the huge Andes mountain range running down the western side. The people living there 8,000 years ago, in what is now Peru and Bolivia, started farming a new type of wild plant: the potato, a remarkably adaptable crop that grows even in cold mountain regions.

Potatoes are brilliant. They are jam-packed with energy, starch and vitamins. And these ancient Andeans figured out how to freeze potatoes for long-term storage. They left them outside to freeze at night, then jumped on them to squash out the water, then froze them again, then dried them in the sun. Amazingly, these dried-out spuds (known as *chuño*) could be kept for over ten years without rotting, which was a lifesaving back-up if the maize (corn) harvest failed. All they had to do to make the chuño edible was add water – yup, even in the Stone Age, people had instant mash! Today, thousands of years later, chuño is still a big part of Peruvian cooking.

Stored for ten years and still delicious!

YUCK! I forgot to freeze mine!

35 SOFA

While you're enjoying your salty snack, you may as well make yourself comfy. Certainly, when you get as old as me, you will welcome a nice sit-down! You may even make a little sound, like "Aaaah, that's better!" when you plonk yourself down on the sofa. The word *sofa* comes from the Arabic *suffah*, meaning a place of shelter or comfort – but sitting hasn't always been about being comfy...

SITTING SEIZA

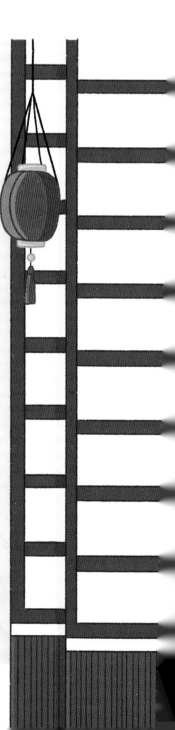

In Europe and North America, it's long been normal to sit on furniture – chairs, sofas, benches, stools, etc. But in East Asia, people have traditionally been more comfortable down on the floor, perhaps sitting on *tatami* mats made of straw and rushes. For centuries, the polite Japanese way of sitting has been called *seiza*. These days, there are different styles that are more relaxed or more appropriate to certain situations, such as the cross-legged *agura* style, or the *tatehiza* pose with one knee raised, which was used by samurai warriors. You might sit like that quite often.

The most important pose of seiza – used in very polite situations to show respect to others – is to sit on the knees with feet folded underneath, so your bottom is cupped by your ankles. You must have a very straight back and not fidget! Bending your joints like this is painful if you haven't done it your whole life, and it's tricky to do in tight trousers. Today, seiza is less common in Japan, except during formal tea ceremonies. But many people still like to sit on the floor.

POTATO CRISPS

You've made it home and all that cycling has left you feeling peckish, so it's time for an afternoon snack. I recommend a healthy bit of fruit, but you might prefer a packet of crisps (known as chips in the USA). These are very common potato snacks today, but did you know the humble spud has a really long and surprising history?

PERU'S POTATOES

If you look at a map of South America, you'll see the huge Andes mountain range running down the western side. The people living there 8,000 years ago, in what is now Peru and Bolivia, started farming a new type of wild plant: the potato, a remarkably adaptable crop that grows even in cold mountain regions.

Potatoes are brilliant. They are jam-packed with energy, starch and vitamins. And these ancient Andeans figured out how to freeze potatoes for long-term storage. They left them outside to freeze at night, then jumped on them to squash out the water, then froze them again, then dried them in the sun. Amazingly, these dried-out spuds (known as *chuño*) could be kept for over ten years without rotting, which was a lifesaving back-up if the maize (corn) harvest failed. All they had to do to make the chuño edible was add water – yup, even in the Stone Age, people had instant mash! Today, thousands of years later, chuño is still a big part of Peruvian cooking.

Stored for ten years and still delicious!

YUCK! I forgot to freeze mine!

95

POTATO PANIC!

Around 800 years ago, Peru became home to the powerful Inka (or Inca) Empire. But in the 1530s, Spanish invaders – known as *conquistadors* – defeated the Inka and brought various foods back to Europe from the Americas. Surprisingly, the delicious potato was not welcome!

A Swiss plant expert called Gaspard Bauhin decided the newly arrived spud looked suspicious. Why was it all lumpy and gnarly? Clearly, he thought, it must cause a terrible disease called leprosy! Oh, and also farting! Yes, many rich people considered the potato to be unsafe to eat, meaning it was mostly fed to animals and very poor people.

Sorry, Gilbert, potatoes make me fart.

But you haven't eaten any!

It wasn't me!

WHO INVENTED CRISPS? MYTHBUSTER!

Let's talk about crisps. Who first decided to slice potatoes thinly and fry them? A famous story says that they were invented in 1853 by a restaurant cook named George Crum in Saratoga Springs, New York, USA. One day a very rich client, Cornelius Vanderbilt, complained that his French fries were too thick. Crum got annoyed and sliced them super thin to mock Vanderbilt, but Vanderbilt loved them! Word spread, and everyone came to eat Crum's super-thin chips.

Fun story, right? Sadly, it's just NOT TRUE! Vanderbilt wasn't even in the country at the time. This story came along many years later, and, even if Crum had sarcastically sliced his chips for some other customer, there had already been several recipes for potato crisps published in cookery books since 1817. Crum was a real guy, but he wasn't a potato pioneer. Never mind, moving on!

Having been freshly cooked in kitchens for a century, dried crisps were first sold in packets and tins in the early 1910s, and in 1920 a chap called Frank Smith was the first to add salt. This is what makes crisps an unhealthy snack, not least because the saltiness makes you want to eat more and more! Flavoured crisps arrived in the 1950s, with the UK and Ireland getting both Salt & Vinegar and Cheese & Onion, while Americans could enjoy BBQ Sauce flavour.

PARMENTIER'S POTATO PSYCHOLOGY

But hang on: how did we get to crisps if Europeans thought potatoes were dangerous? We have a spud superhero to thank! Antoine-Augustin Parmentier was a French food researcher who had eaten potatoes as a prisoner of war, and he'd suffered neither leprosy nor farts! In 1772, he showed scientists that potatoes were safe, but he needed to convince ordinary people. So he did some clever potato publicity stunts.

He hosted a dinner party for the French royal family and celebrities, where all the courses looked like other food, but were made of potato. He even asked the Queen to wear potato flowers in her hair. But his best trick was a cheeky "reverse psychology" prank on peasants near Paris. Parmentier planted potatoes in a field guarded by soldiers, then told the peasants this was special royal food and they weren't allowed any. At night-time, he told the soldiers to leave their posts, hoping that the naughty peasants would sneak out to dig up the posh people's potatoes. Sure enough, they did! And they soon realised this was a food fit for humans, not just horses.

Thanks to Parmentier, the potato went from dreaded to delicious, and by the 1800s many ordinary people were eating them. They became a very important crop in Ireland, which sadly led to a horrible disaster. In 1845, a nasty plant disease called *blight* swept through the country, making all the potatoes go rotten. A million people died of starvation, while another million refugees were forced to move to other countries. It was a terrible tragedy, and it remains a very painful story for Irish people today.

35 SOFA

While you're enjoying your salty snack, you may as well make yourself comfy. Certainly, when you get as old as me, you will welcome a nice sit-down! You may even make a little sound, like "Aaaah, that's better!" when you plonk yourself down on the sofa. The word *sofa* comes from the Arabic *suffah*, meaning a place of shelter or comfort – but sitting hasn't always been about being comfy...

SITTING SEIZA

In Europe and North America, it's long been normal to sit on furniture – chairs, sofas, benches, stools, etc. But in East Asia, people have traditionally been more comfortable down on the floor, perhaps sitting on *tatami* mats made of straw and rushes. For centuries, the polite Japanese way of sitting has been called *seiza*. These days, there are different styles that are more relaxed or more appropriate to certain situations, such as the cross-legged *agura* style, or the *tatehiza* pose with one knee raised, which was used by samurai warriors. You might sit like that quite often.

The most important pose of seiza – used in very polite situations to show respect to others – is to sit on the knees with feet folded underneath, so your bottom is cupped by your ankles. You must have a very straight back and not fidget! Bending your joints like this is painful if you haven't done it your whole life, and it's tricky to do in tight trousers. Today, seiza is less common in Japan, except during formal tea ceremonies. But many people still like to sit on the floor.

RECLINE LIKE A ROMAN

In taverns and restaurants, ancient Greeks and Romans sat upright in chairs. But when eating at home, the very rich ones reclined on their side and grabbed food with their right hand. In fact, the word *recline* – which now means lying on our backs – comes from the Greek *kline*, meaning a long couch for sideways sitting.

This style of posh lounging wasn't meant to be comfy at all. Instead, it was meant to show a person's bodily control, as proof to the other guests that they were masters of dignity and decorum. Well, that was until they did a huge burp or choked on a grape!

Not everyone can lounge with dignity!

SEATS OF POWER

Help, I'm scared of heights!

In your home, everyone's chair is probably the same, but 500 years ago in England, a wealthy man might have a bigger chair than his wife and kids, who sat on backless stools. And of course, the most impressive chairs of all are royal thrones.

Nearly 400 years ago, Shah Jahan – who built the Taj Mahal and was the mighty ruler of the Mughal Empire in South Asia – sat in an extremely beautiful *Peacock throne* covered in gold, jewels and gorgeous peacock designs. And 1,000 years ago, the Byzantine emperor in his palace in Constantinople (now Istanbul in Turkey) had a mechanical throne that rose up in the air, as if it were a special effects prop in a West End musical! This made the ruler seem closer to heaven than everyone else. I wonder if it ever got stuck and they had to get a ladder to help them down. We don't know!

Er, how do we get him down?

In the 1600s, King Louis XIV of France decided that only his chairs were allowed to have armrests. If King Louis were alive today and you went to the cinema with him, he'd definitely hog the shared cup-holder!

NEVER SIT ON THE GOLDEN STOOL!

Not all thrones were for sitting on. In the early 1700s, the mighty warrior Osei Kofi Tutu I conquered his rivals in West Africa (modern-day Ghana), and founded a kingdom called the Asante Empire. To symbolise the new nation, the king's chief priest, Okomfo Anokye, is said to have summoned a beautiful golden stool from the skies. It was so precious that nobody could sit on it. It rested on an animal-skin rug and had its own umbrella to protect it from the sun. Ceremonial stools became very important in Asante culture, but the Golden Stool was the most important of all. Known as *Sika Dwa Kofi* (the Golden Stool Born on a Friday), it was almost treated like a king itself.

In the 1800s, the British Empire tried to conquer the Asante Empire, and eventually succeeded on the third attempt. In 1900, rumours spread that the British officer in charge, Frederick Hodgson, wanted to sit on the sacred stool. The Asante rose up in anger, and this conflict became known as the War of the Golden Stool. Though the Asante lost, they managed to hide the stool from Hodgson, so he never got to park his unwanted bum on it.

No one comes near the stool.

Shhh... Don't tell my husband, but I really fancy the Duke.

But I AM your husband!

GREG'S GREATEST

GOSSIPING CHAIR

History is crammed with loads of fascinating furniture (did you know the ancient Greeks had highchairs for feeding their babies?), but one of my faves was the *Canapé confident* from France in the 1700s. This was a fancy sofa for fancy people, designed for gossiping and flirting. The idea was that two people who weren't supposed to be chatting would sit on the sofa facing in different directions, so it looked as though they were talking to other people. They could then whisper their cheeky secrets to each other without anyone getting suspicious. I imagine this would be a lot of fun in your school classroom, but I'm not sure your teacher would be too impressed...

A REFRESHING DRINK

If you're having a salty snack, you might also need a drink – it's important to stay hydrated! Personally, I prefer a simple glass of water or a nice mug of milky tea, because I find the sweetness of many soft drinks makes my teeth go all fizzy. Sweet soft drinks are nothing new, and even boring old water isn't as boring as it sounds!

THE JOYS OF SPRING WATER

Natural spring water that comes bubbling up from the ground has often been drunk as medicine. In ancient China, around 1,500 years ago, there was a hot spring on the Shahe River, in Henan Province, where the water was so hot people could cook rice in it! Even though it sounds like it might have burnt their tongues, local Taoist monks would drink from the waters if they didn't feel very well, and, apparently, they would be healed after 40 days.

I grew up in a town called Tunbridge Wells that became famous in the early 1600s for its natural spring, even though the water trickled out a dirty orange colour and tasted terrible – like someone had left a bunch of rusty nails in an old watering can. The water was naturally rich in iron, which people believed made it a great medical cure, meaning snoozy little Tunbridge Wells was transformed into a booming tourist hotspot. In fact, in the early 1900s, King Edward VII visited on holiday, and that's why my hometown gets to be all fancy-schmancy by calling itself *Royal* Tunbridge Wells. Sadly, this doesn't make me an honorary prince, even though I keep asking.

HOT! HOT!

Rice, anyone?

WERE PEOPLE WATER-DODGERS?

Often history books will say that people in the past didn't drink water because it was dirty and dangerous, so they drank alcohol instead. Well, this isn't strictly true. Yes, many different societies preferred to drink tea and weak alcoholic drinks (like ale, wine, honey mead, fermented milk, etc.), but sometimes this was because these drinks had extra *calories* in them, which gave people more energy. In truth, we know loads of people drank water in the past, though they certainly had to be careful their water wasn't coming from the same place they emptied their potty!

ADDING BUBBLES

Have you ever wondered who first figured out how to make fizzy drinks? We can thank the brilliantly brainy English scientist Joseph Priestley (the same dude who named the rubber eraser) for this research.

Priestley lived around the time when the gas carbon dioxide was first discovered. Interested, he popped to a nearby brewery to watch the gas being released during the beer-making process. It made him curious. In 1767, he started experimenting with acid and chalk and, in 1772, he published his new scientific method for making carbonated – or fizzy – water, which he hoped would be a cure for all sorts of diseases. Funnily enough, because his invention required a pig's bladder to store the water, a rival inventor said Priestley's fizzy water tasted of pig's wee! Priestley was not amused.

A few years later, in 1783, a chap called Johann Jacob Schweppe used this research to sell his own fizzy drink. And, nearly 250 years later, his company is still going, though obviously *he's* not still going … fizzy water might have been considered good for your health, but not THAT good!

And here's the fresh pig bladder...

SWEET AND SOUR FRUITY FLAVOURS

One of my fave drinks is homemade raspberry lemonade with a mint leaf bunged on top (to make me look extra classy). People have been making delicious fruity soft drinks for absolutely ages. Simple lemonade can be traced back a thousand years to medieval Egypt, where sugarcane was added to sweeten sour lemons.

But there are even older drinks that combine a sugary zing with the sharp tang at the back of the mouth. Over 2,500 years ago, the Scythians, who were nomadic (wandering) horse-riders in what is now Siberia and Central Asia, drank a thick syrup made of sour cherry, which they called *askhu*.

Needs more sugarcane!

GREG'S GREATEST

HISTORICAL REFRESHMENT

In Iran you can drink a thousand-year-old recipe called *sekanjabin* or *sharbat* (where we get the word *sherbet*). This is a tasty mix of sweet honey and sour vinegar, sometimes flavoured with fruit, mint or rose petals. Just like Priestley's fizzy water, it was thought to be good for one's health. Because it was drunk in very hot places, it was usually served with crushed ice, making it a medieval slushie.

UNHEALTHY HEALTH DRINKS

The world's most popular soft drink is Coca-Cola. It's tasty, but not very good for us (or our teeth). But when it was first invented in 1886, it was actually sold as a health syrup. Its creator was John Stith Pemberton, who lived in Atlanta, Georgia, in the USA. He distilled leaves from a coca plant, added caffeine and sugar, and sold his syrup at a local pharmacy. It didn't sell well, and customers had to add the fizzy water themselves.

Pemberton's friend, Frank Robinson, then came up with Coca-Cola's famous name and logo, but it still wasn't a big success until Pemberton sold the company to the savvy businessman Asa G. Candler. This fella knew how to market a product, and claimed it would cure people's headaches and tiredness. He also said the recipe was a secret, which made it sound mega exciting. Who doesn't love a mystery?!

MONEY

Your fizzy drink isn't a freebie. You might have raided the fridge for it, but someone in your family had to buy it first. That meant handing over money. But what *is* money, anyway? Weirdly, it can be anything, so long as everyone agrees it's money! And history is full of surprising examples...

PAID BY SPADE

If I were to pop down to my garden shed, I wouldn't shout "I'm rich!" when I saw my spade. But that's because I don't live during China's "Warring States Period". You see, 2,700 years ago, violent rebellions broke out, and this political chaos forced the ruling Zhou Dynasty to make new types of cash that looked like either a spade, a knife or a bridge.

Spade money looked like a garden trowel without a handle, Knife money resembled a blunt chopping knife, and Bridge money curved like a humpback bridge. Slowly, these big hunks of shaped metal shrank to the size of coins, but kept their unique design – fascinating, right?

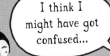

I think I might have got confused...

GREG'S GREATEST

That'll be three silver coins.

How about this useless iron bar instead? No...?

WORTHLESS MONEY

Here's a funny story which might be untrue! Around 2,500 years ago, the ancient Greek Spartans wanted to stop people being greedy, so a politician called Lycurgus banned gold and silver, and said iron bars were the new cash. But people melted the iron to make other things, so the government said "Oi! Stop that!" and damaged the iron with vinegar, so it became useless. This meant they couldn't buy anything from foreigners because ... well, the Spartans were trying to pay with rusty metal!

YOU OWE ME ONE BOULDER!

For centuries, people on the islands of Yap – which belong to the Federated States of Micronesia in the middle of the Pacific Ocean – have used thousands of stone discs, with holes cut in the middle, as a type of money called *Rai stones*. Some of these discs are very small, but others are absolutely massive and weigh several tonnes! In fact, these ones cannot be moved, so when people agree to trade one, the ownership changes, but it stays exactly where it is.

Rai stones are fascinating because their value is based on how difficult they were to dig up on an island called Palau. Obviously, the heavier ones were much harder to transport in a canoe, so those are worth more. But if someone turned up today with a mechanical digger and easily dug out a monster-sized stone, it wouldn't be worth as much as a dinky one dug by hand, because using a digger would be cheating! It's the effort, not the size, that matters.

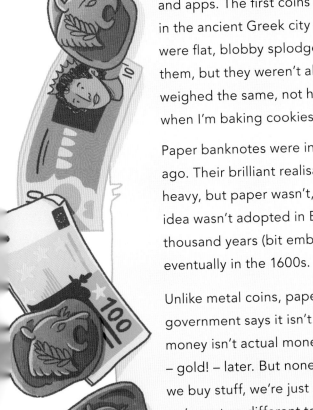

COINS AND CASH

Of course, it's very hard to insert a four-tonne stone disc into a vending machine. Instead, we use coins, paper money, bank cards and apps. The first coins were probably invented 2,600 years ago in the ancient Greek city of Lydia (in modern-day Turkey). These were flat, blobby splodges of gold with lion designs stamped on them, but they weren't all the same shape; what mattered was they weighed the same, not how they looked. I make the same excuse when I'm baking cookies and they come out all wrong...

Paper banknotes were invented by the Chinese, about 1,200 years ago. Their brilliant realisation was that coins (and spades) were heavy, but paper wasn't, so it was easier to carry. This ingenious idea wasn't adopted in Europe or North America for nearly one thousand years (bit embarrassing for us…), but we got there eventually in the 1600s.

Unlike metal coins, paper money is totally worthless unless the government says it isn't. This is a system called *fiat* currency. Paper money isn't actual money at all, it's a promise to pay the real money – gold! – later. But none of us have any gold, do we? Nope, when we buy stuff, we're just moving imaginary money around, meaning we're not so different to the Spartans with their pointless iron bars. Isn't money weird?

38 BOARD GAMES

Evening is drawing in, so time for a bit of family bonding – or maybe squabbling! I love a board game. There's something really fun about shocking everyone with a surprise move you've been planning for ages. As you can tell, I'm quite a sneaky gamer. But did you know that people have been battling over board games for 5,000 years?

BRONZE AGE GAMING

Yes, the earliest board games seem to date back to the Bronze Age, with archaeologists having found beautiful gaming boards from ancient Egypt and Mesopotamia (modern Iraq). Egyptian royals and nobles loved playing a game called *Senet*, where they had to get their pieces from one end of a narrow rectangular board to the other, throwing knucklebones as ancient dice to decide which pieces to move, and how far. Modern experts think the game was perhaps meant to represent the journey to the Egyptian afterlife, getting past all the scary gods and obstacles.

The Mesopotamian version, known as the *Royal Game of Ur*, was similar, but the board was narrow in the middle – only one space wide – making it trickier to get across. It gradually seems to have inspired backgammon, which is still played today. I guess some ideas never go out of fashion.

WAR GAMES

Chess probably dates back around 1,500 years to ancient India, where it was called *Chaturanga*. When it reached the Middle East, maybe 1,300 years ago, it took its famous new name, chess (meaning "king" in Persian, because you must capture your opponent's king). It was played to practise battlefield strategy, because it's all about outwitting your enemy. It is a game of murderous slaughter, but without any actual violence (hopefully!).

Chess isn't unique, though. In Africa, there are many turn-based, two-player strategy board games which have their own names but are grouped together as *Mancala* games. In Ghana, *Oware* is played with 48 seeds; the two players move their 24 seeds into 12 pots, and "sow" them like a farmer. Their opponent must capture 25 seeds to win the game. It's less violent than chess!

But, sticking with chess, how did it get so popular? 1,100 years ago, a huge Islamic empire called the Umayyad Caliphate ruled over the Middle East, North Africa and Spain. Chess soon spread through these lands. Back then, Spain was called *Al-Andalus* in Arabic, and the Muslims living there were called *Moors* by their Christian enemies. Despite the religious rivalry, chess spread from Moorish Spain to wider Europe. It also went eastwards from the Middle East into Japan, China and eventually Russia. Everyone wanted to play!

Drat! Don't suppose we can play cards instead?

GREG'S GREATEST

CHESS GAME

One of my fave medieval stories (WARNING: it might not be true!) is from about 950 years ago. It says that the fate of Seville, a city in southern Spain, was decided by a chess match. When the Christian king Alfonso VI of Castile attacked the Muslims living there, the Muslim poet Muhammad Ibn-Ammar challenged him to a game of chess. Whoever won got the city. Luckily, Ibn-Ammar was a chess master, and Alfonso was forced to go home. Nice story, right? If only we could decide modern wars with a quick game of Snap!

ELEPHANTS OR BISHOPS?

Medieval Europeans loved chess, but they changed some of the pieces. The Persian game had a piece shaped like a chariot, but in Europe that became a rook (castle), while the Persian *vizier* (chief minister) was swapped for a queen. Most amusing of all, the Persians had an elephant piece, but Europeans didn't have elephants on their battlefields, so swapped it for a bishop. How is a religious bishop the same as an elephant?! I would be very offended if I were a bishop!

The most famous medieval chess pieces were found on the Scottish island of Lewis. These beautiful pieces were carved from walrus ivory and whales' teeth by Viking craftspeople in Norway, about 800 years ago. What I love most about them are the hilarious expressions on the warriors' faces, particularly the guy who is biting his shield like an angry dog chomping on a slipper!

That looks nothing like me!

THE WINNER TAKES IT ALL

A craze for new board games arose in the 1800s, particularly in Britain. Many were designed to teach kids about the stages of life, or geography, or the British Empire. They were fun, but educational. Funnily enough, sometimes the message got a bit lost. Take Monopoly: you might enjoy feeling super rich and buying loads of hotels, but the game was actually invented by an American woman named Lizzie Magie, who believed modern life was unfair and the rich got away with too much.

She created The Landlord's Game in 1903, and it had two sets of rules. You could either play so that everyone did well, or so that one person ended up owning everything (which is called having a monopoly). Lizzie hoped people would see that the first system was fairer. Her game became popular in universities and one day a man named Charles Darrow played it. He preferred the selfish version, and cheekily claimed to have invented it himself! Darrow became a millionaire selling Lizzie's idea to a toy company, but she got only a few hundred dollars. How's that for an unfair monopoly?

VIDEO GAMES

We play board games with others, but sometimes it's fun to play games on our own. That's why I enjoy video games. Chances are you love them too, because they let you perform amazing stunts, fight battles, explore entire worlds or even build them yourself! Obviously, high-tech video games don't go back very far into the past – if you'd wanted to play *Minecraft* back then, you'd have had to go to your nearest stone quarry and start swinging an actual pickaxe! But video games are older than you might expect. In fact, even your great-grandparents might have played them.

NIMATRON

The first ever games machine was built by the American nuclear physicist Edward Condon, all the way back in 1940 – yup, arcade games are as old as the Second World War. It was called the Nimatron, and it was a powerful computer built to play what some people claim is an ancient Chinese game called Nim (or *Jian-Shizi*). It's a tricky game of mathematical strategy – there are sixteen sticks stacked in a pyramid, with seven in the bottom row, five in the third row, three in the second row, and one stick at the top. Two players take it in turns to pick up any number of sticks from a single row. The loser is whoever has to pick up the last stick. Simple? Yes. Easy? Nope!

Condon's Nimatron machine was displayed at the World's Fair in New York. There were no sticks this time: the aim was to turn off illuminated bulbs. Of the 100,000 people who played against the machine, only 10,000 won the game.

BRAND NEW

NIMATRON!

ARCADE PARADE

The Nimatron was so ahead of its time, nothing else came along until the late 1960s. In 1972, a company called Atari launched very successful arcade games machines, which were installed in bars, chain restaurants, bowling alleys and amusement parks. These machines were coin-operated, so you had to pay to play, and the game was called *PONG*, which was basically digital ping-pong. People could either take on the computer or battle a friend. Everyone was desperate to get the highest score and see their name at the top of the leader-board.

GAMING AT HOME

Of course, if you want to play games at home, you don't have to insert a coin every time (unless your family are REALLY stingy…). Actually, even in the 1960s and '70s people didn't always have to go out to arcades if they fancied a quick button-bashing session. Yes, the first ever home gaming system was created in 1967. It had two hand-held controls, offered quite a few games (including golf and laser shooting, which needed special attachments) and was a very exciting technology. Unfortunately, it was called *The Brown Box*, which … well, was a totally rubbish name! Talk about dull, right? It was relaunched in 1972 under the much snazzier name of *Magnavox Odyssey* – ooh yeah, now you're talking! But the most popular early home gaming system was made by Atari. Their 2600 model went into two million American homes in 1980 and started a gaming revolution.

Aw, Mum, I didn't want THIS kind of brown box!

GAMING TOGETHER

Maybe you play multiplayer games online? Well, that's not new either. Back in the 1970s – before the internet was even invented, and waaaaay before super-speedy Wi-Fi – a game called *Empire* allowed up to 30 players to join together in a space shoot-'em-up adventure. The game ran on a computing system called PLATO, which was networked across lots of machines, so people in universities – where expensive computers were available for students and staff – could play against people in different cities. This was the beginning of massive multiplayer online games, though these were more like *mini* multiplayer online games.

BRILLIANT BESTSELLERS

One of the most popular games on the revolutionary Atari 2600 was called *Space Invaders*, and it was quite similar to the shooty-bang-bang multiplayer *Empire*. But then came two huge games that broke with the fashion for war games. The first was *Pac-Man* in 1980, an amazingly addictive Japanese game where a bright yellow, pie-shaped character moves around a maze, hungrily chomping pellets while being chased by evil ghosts. I realise that makes zero sense, but who says games need to be logical, anyway?

The second game was called *Tetris*. The player has to move and rotate weirdly shaped blocks falling from the sky to fit them into different gaps. *Tetris* was designed in 1984 as a secret hobby by a Russian software engineer named Alexey Pajitnov. It was never meant to be popular, but it was soon passed around Moscow by its fans, and, just like chess in medieval times, *Tetris* gradually spread around the world. The problem was, this was during the so-called Cold War, when the Communist Soviet Union (now Russia) was the enemy of the USA and UK. Indeed, in the USA *Tetris* was loudly marketed as a very, very Russian game, with a famous Russian cathedral shown on the box.

> We're at war with Russia! We must not play their games... Oooh, this is fun though!

Luckily, *Tetris* became the property of the Japanese company Nintendo, which made things easier. They released *Tetris* on the hand-held Nintendo Game Boy machine in 1989, and added a beepy electronic version of a famous Russian folk song called "Korobeiniki". As soon as you started the game, this brilliantly catchy tune would play over and over on a loop, until it lodged in your brain FOR EVER! Seriously, I haven't played *Tetris* in 30 years, and I'm humming it right now: *Doo doodoodoo doodoodoo doodoodoo doo doo doo doo doo doo doo doo doo...* See? I told you!

So, while you are lucky to be living in a time of amazingly realistic video games, sometimes the old ones are the best.

40 THERMOSTAT

You finish your gaming session and you suddenly realise you feel rather chilly. Someone must have nudged the thermostat, because it's freezing in here! Luckily, one of the most obvious differences between modern life and the past is the way our homes are easily returned to a nice temperature. We can turn the heating up in the winter, or switch on air conditioners and electric fans in the summer. But, even without electrical gadgets, people in the past also found ways to change the temp.

HYPOCAUST

The ancient Romans were master engineers, and one of their sweetest gimmicks was the *hypocaust*. This was some seriously impressive underfloor heating, created by building a basement made of brick pillars with lots of gaps in-between. In it would be a large furnace, probably manned by enslaved servants, whose job was to chuck fuel onto the fire. The heat would be directed into the rooms above by chimney flues, or would simply waft between the brick pillars to warm the bottom of the floor tiles. Ooh, how toasty!

This wasn't solely a Roman idea. In fact, it was widely used in parts of East Asia too. The ancient Koreans used an elaborate technique called *ondol*, where a floor made of clay tiles had a long flue or pipe under it. This transported heat from the next room (usually the kitchen) along the underside of the whole house, warming the floor, then up and out of a chimney. In China, the *kang* was similar but the only section that was heated was a small, raised clay platform on which people might relax or snooze.

Toasty!

EXPLODING HOUSES!

In the 1800s, heating technology became more about large metal contraptions. In Europe and North America, rich people began installing large heating stoves. These were cast-iron chambers with a roaring fire inside, which could pump heat into a nearby room, or send it elsewhere through long pipes. But the best way to spread warm air through a room was with a new American invention called a *radiator*, which showed up in the 1840s. These were wide and chunky metal objects made up of lots of connected tubes, with the hot water rushing through them and the heat wafting out into the room.

However, safety was a big problem. You might remember from earlier in the book that showers in the 1800s could burn people if the water was overheated? Well, some of these boilers relied on very high-pressure steam, and if the pipes weren't strong enough then they could burst like an overinflated balloon, flattening the whole house in a terrible blast. Sadly, creature comforts in the past could be deadly dangerous.

THE PUNKHAWALA FAN FLAPPERS

Until 1947, South Asia was ruled by the British. The posh colonials living there wanted to keep cool in the summers. To do this, they relied upon their Indian servants to hang a very large piece of *punkah* cloth from the ceiling. It was a bit like a ship's sail, attached to a pulley system with a rope at the end.

The tough task of the *punkhawala* was to pull the rope back and forth, for up to eight hours per shift. This wafted a gentle breeze inside the house, so the rich Brits could stay comfortable. However, the unlucky punkah-pullers were stuck outside, suffering in the sweltering sun.

Old photos show them lying down with the rope tied around their waist, so it couldn't slip out of their hands. It was a horrid job. They were treated as racially inferior to the British, and their pay was so low they often needed a second job. Imagine being that tired, and lying down in the sunshine – you'd fall asleep, right? Sadly, if punkhawalas did that, they'd be beaten and kicked by their bosses. Awful.

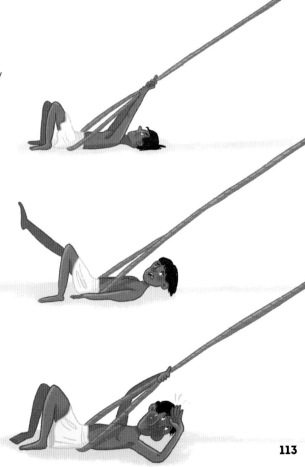

ANCIENT AIR CONDITIONING

Many modern buildings have air conditioning. These electricity-powered machines were first sold to the public in the early 1900s, but there had been many earlier attempts to overcome a sweaty situation.

Perhaps the most impressive was in ancient China, where the emperor's engineers built machines to cool the massive rooms in his palaces. These machines were very large rotating fans with seven wheels, which were spun by servants pushing or cranking them. However, by the mid-700s (during the famous Tang Dynasty), these fans were re-engineered to be powered by water fountains instead, so the servants could go do something else.

I'm a big fan of this big fan.

Some ancient solutions were simpler, but still effective. The ancient Egyptians took papyrus reeds, soaked them in water from the Nile, and then hung them in their windows. When the breeze wafted through, it sprinkled cool water vapour into the rooms, making people feel like they were being gently spritzed. However, there was also a much smarter architectural trick available – the *wind catcher*. This technology is maybe 5,000 years old, but, amazingly, it's still used in Egypt and the Middle East because it's way more environmentally friendly than using loads of electricity to power air-conditioning units. So, how does it work?

A wind catcher can come in different designs – it might look like a tower with holes in it, or a downward-sloping flap, or lots of arms sticking out of a tall block. It is mounted on top of buildings in hot, desert climates, and it catches the cool breeze from the desert and directs the airflow down into the building. Not only does this deliver a refreshing indoor breeze, it also pushes out the hot air and cools the sun-facing bricks in the outer walls. All in all, this clever design stops the whole building (and the people in it) from feeling like chickens being roasted in an oven!

Cool design, dude.

Literally!

THE TIN CAN

Your tummy is gurgling – it must be getting close to dinner time! If you peer into your kitchen cupboard, you'll see all sorts of food and utensils with their own fascinating histories. One of the least famous, but most interesting, stories is how the humble tin can was invented to help the French army win wars. Except it didn't quite go to plan...

grumble

grumble

CAN-DO ATTITUDE

For thousands of years, armies at war needed to either steal food from nearby fields, or resupply themselves with regular deliveries. This was tricky if they were far from home, as food couldn't be stored for long and might go mouldy after only a few days. Meat had to be heavily salted, and sailors often had to eat dry, salty biscuits called *hard tack*. Yuck!

In 1795, the French government thought "This is silly!", so they ran a competition offering a big cash prize to whoever could make food last longer. In 1809, Nicolas Appert stepped forward to collect the reward. He was a *confectioner* who preserved sweet fruits in jelly, and his clever solution was to seal food in glass jars and then boil it (killing the bacteria inside). Funnily enough, Appert had no clue why his idea worked – nobody understood how bacteria affected food yet.

Of course, glass jars aren't ideal for warzones: they shatter if dropped, and they can explode if you overheat them! Step forward ingenious inventor Philippe de Girard, who switched glass for metal cans. However, because France had lots of annoying rules about making money from inventions, Girard secretly travelled to Britain – France's enemy at the time – to sell his idea. It was bought by Peter Durand, who then sold it to a factory owner called Bryan Donkin.

Soon, Donkin was making tin cans for the British army and navy. And who did the British fight in 1815? Yup, the French! An invention sponsored by the French to help them win wars ended up helping the British defeat them at the Battle of Waterloo – oops! But it also led to a revolution in food storage that changed the world.

Hey, that's ours – copycats!

4₂ FRIDGE-FREEZER

We live in a world where many people can get any type of food at any time of year. In fact, right now, I'm eating delicious, juicy grapes, even though I'm writing this in the winter! How come? It's because we have global transport networks (planes, trains, ships, trucks) which can quickly deliver stuff from the other side of the planet before it goes all rotten and mouldy. Most of the food is refrigerated during transport, so bacteria cannot grow. We do the same thing at home with our fridge-freezer. But people used to find other ways to keep their food fresh.

SUNDRIED SNACKS

In parts of Africa, such as Nigeria, it has long been traditional to dry grains in the sunshine by laying them out on a mat or on the roof. This is called *solarisation*. The idea isn't to give your dinner a suntan, but rather to stop it rotting by removing moisture. Handily, it also kills any sneaky insects laying their eggs, because nobody wants bugs squirming in their delicious Ogi pudding! Farmers also sometimes dangle crops in big bunches from trees, poles or the roof of a barn, or hang them inside bins made of straw. These techniques are all very ancient, but still work well today.

A BIG PINCH OF SALT

Do you salt your food? I'm guessing you sprinkle some on your dinner if it tastes a bit bland, right? But that's not what I mean by salting! No, I'm talking about preventing a nasty bout of food poisoning. Before people had fridges, adding salt to meat helped dry it out, so bacteria couldn't grow. That meant some salted meat could last for YEARS! Roman soldiers liked to carry salted Lucanian sausages in their knapsacks as a marching snack. Meanwhile, the ancient Egyptians pickled various animals in salt water. No need for sell-by dates back then.

For several thousand years, the many different Indigenous peoples of North America have eaten *pemmican*, which is meat from a moose, deer, elk, cow or bison. Instead of salting, the meat is sliced into thin strips, dried in the sunshine, then pounded into powdery flakes. This is mixed with melted animal fats and tasty wild berries, and stored in leather bags to harden. Pemmican is so full of protein and energy that it was copied by European fur traders in Canada, and was later taken by European explorers to the frozen lands of the Arctic and Antarctic.

Ooh! Can I have some pemmican?

Of course you pemmican-can!

INGENIOUS ICE HOUSES

Your freezer may look shiny and new, but the idea isn't. Evidence from Bronze Age Mesopotamia (Iraq) suggests that people stored ice in special buildings 3,800 years ago. And if we jump to 2,400 years ago, the ancient Persians were experts at digging underground pits with a cone-shaped building over the top. These were called *yakhchals* and they stored ice delivered from the mountains. But the Persians could also use them to make their own ice, which is way harder! They did this by cooling water overnight using wind catchers (remember them?). The yakhchal's internal temperature gradually became sub-zero, thanks to the chunky mudbrick walls blocking out the sun's heat.

You said this job was nice and easy!

No, I said *ice and wheezy!*

This clever technique meant ice could be sold throughout the medieval world, and by the 1600s ice houses had arrived in Britain, particularly in rich people's gardens. Huge ones were also built under major cities, so ice could be sold to shops and restaurants. In fact, in the 1800s, you could get ice delivered to your house by the iceman – that guy literally had the coolest job!

43 CUTLERY

At last, it's dinner time, which usually means sitting down for some tasty food. Chances are, when that food isn't in your mouth, it's in a serving dish or sitting on plates or in bowls. For billions of people around the world, this *crockery* is totally normal. Even people in the late Stone Age ate some of their food out of clay bowls. But what you use to cut up your food, and how you deliver it to your gaping gob, is a more complicated story.

FINGER FOOD

Perhaps history's most common cutlery was no cutlery at all! Billions of people have chosen to eat with their fingers (including the ancient Romans, Jews, Babylonians and Egyptians), and it continues today in many modern nations. Eating with the hands is often said to make food a more pleasurable experience, and easier to share. It's common to only use the right hand, however, because the left hand is for wiping one's bottom.

But it's tricky to gulp down hot soup with your hands, so it's no surprise archaeologists have found what look like spoons made from seashells, from tens of thousands of years ago. Interestingly, the Romans had a spoon called a *cochlearium*, and *cochlear* was their word for a snail shell. Coincidence? Maybe not!

A LOT OF FUSS OVER FORKS

Along with spoons, knives are properly old! They go back to the slicing tools of the very, very, VERY early Stone Age, two million years ago. In medieval times, most European people carried a multi-purpose knife on their belt, and used it to chop up their dinner. Yes, if you were invited to a meal at someone's house, you were expected to provide your own cutlery. I'm pretty sure my friends would be shocked if I turned up wearing a belt of forks...

Actually, forks have often been rather shocking. For most of history, they were only used for holding meat while it was carved, not for pronging it into your mouth. When Princess Theophano of the Byzantine Empire (now in Turkey) arrived to marry her German husband, Prince Otto, in 972, everyone was appalled during the wedding feast when she pulled out a tiny golden fork to eat with – this was considered ridiculous behaviour! Even in the 1300s, most Italians ate spaghetti by scooping it into their mouths with their hands. They did gradually adopt forks, but the English remained way behind – in 1608, when an English writer called Thomas Coryat returned from Italy, his pals mocked him for using a fork at dinner.

Until the 1700s, forks had only two prongs, or *tines*, and they were very straight. Gradually a third was added, and these prongs started to curve, so forks could be used to scoop up food, as well as stab it. In the 1800s, forks with a fourth prong arrived in Europe, yet when the famous writer Charles Dickens toured the USA in the 1840s, he was amazed to see Americans were still using the old, straight, two-pronged fork. He said they looked like sword-swallowers at a circus!

GREG'S GREATEST

CUTLERY CHEMISTRY

Most modern cutlery is made of stainless steel. It was invented in the 1910s, but before that cutlery would be made from tin, copper and brass. These are reactive metals, meaning they have a chemical reaction when they touch anything acidic. Basically, if you cook acidic foods in a copper pan, or eat them with copper cutlery, it can make your dinner taste extra sweet, extra sour or – worst of all – like you're licking a radiator! If you don't want to taste any metal at all, you should invest in a solid gold spoon, because gold doesn't react with acids.

Yuck, radiator!

POISONER!

It's only onions!

CHOP IT UP

In East Asian countries – like China, Vietnam, South Korea and Japan – weird-tasting cutlery isn't a problem because people prefer to use chopsticks to pick up their food. Archaeologists estimate that chopsticks were invented in China around 7,000 years ago, and they seem to have spread to other countries about 1,500 years ago. Early on, they were used as cooking utensils to pick up lumps of meat and vegetables from boiling pans of oil without cooks burning their hands. Ouch! People switched to using them as cutlery about 2,500 years ago, when a fuel shortage crisis made it necessary to chop up food into tiny bitesize chunks, so it needed less firewood to cook it.

Chopsticks are usually made of bamboo, although they were sometimes made of fancy materials like brass, silver, lacquer and beautiful stones called jade and agate. In medieval China, it was believed that silver chopsticks would change colour if an enemy put poison in your dinner. Useful, right? Unfortunately, that's not actually true, but silver *can* change colour if you put garlic or onions in the food, which probably meant some people thought they were being poisoned when they weren't! Awkward...

HEADPHONES

What's your favourite song? How easy is it for you to listen to it right now? I bet you just have to click a couple of buttons, right? You're SO lucky! Back in the 1700s, people might hear their favourite singer only once in their *entire* life! Even a song they had seen performed many times was still impossible to own, because there was no recording technology. Yes, for most of history, if you liked a song you either had to find someone to sing it for you, or learn how to sing it yourself (assuming you didn't have a voice that sounded like a howling cat...).

GOOD VIBRATIONS

That all changed when sound technology arrived. We can thank the famous Thomas Edison (Mr Light Bulb!), who invented the *phonograph* in 1877. It was a super-clever device. Sound is basically the air vibrating, and that was captured by a funnel-shaped horn which sent the vibrations down to be etched into a tinfoil or wax cylinder by a stylus. Hey presto, a recording! To play the sound back, the cylinder was rotated by a crank and the stylus moved through the wax grooves, sending the vibrations back out of the horn. OK, yes, the audio quality was dodgy, and the volume was rubbish – oh, and at first, you could only play a song a few times before it stopped working ... but ... um ... apart from that, it was amazing!

I love this one, play it again!

Er ... I can't!

GRAMOPHONE

Next, in 1887, came Germany's Emile Berliner with his *gramophone*. This sounded a bit better than Edison's machine. This time the music was recorded on flat circular discs made of zinc and wax, instead of cylinders. Oddly, Berliner also sold chocolate records as a novelty gift for children – I mean, I love music, but I'm not sure I want to eat it?!

Gramophones were good, but they still had issues. A musician's performance was captured on a master disc that could only be copied a couple of hundred times before it got too damaged. So, if 10,000 people wanted to buy a song, the musician had to re-record it maybe 50 times! To avoid that, some musicians recorded into several horns at the same time. Cunning, right? Well, it was a bit of a squeeze to cram a whole orchestra into a room as well as loads of big gramophones!

Berliner wasn't just an inventor. He understood marketing too, and cleverly earned success by working with celebrity opera singers, like Enrico Caruso and Dame Nellie Melba. They made stacks of cash with this new technology because everyone wanted to hear them sing (opera was surprisingly popular back then!). Berliner also used a brilliantly memorable advertising image of a small dog looking quizzically at the gramophone, with the caption "His Master's Voice". It's still famous today.

GREG'S GREATEST

COVER VERSIONS

Until the 1920s, sheet music – which is the written instructions telling a musician what notes to play – massively outsold recorded music. Yeah, 100 years before social media helped us enjoy lip-sync videos and bedroom cover versions, people were banging out their own copycat versions on the dining room piano.

LISTENING OUT

Initially, most people couldn't afford a phonograph or gramophone. They instead went to *phonograph parlours* – shops with coin-operated machines, a bit like a games arcade. They held listening tubes up to their ears to hear songs, jokes, cheerful whistling (yes, really!), speeches and whatever else fitted onto the three-minute-long discs. Gradually gramophones became cheaper and people could listen at home, although they had to hand-crank the gramophone to rotate the disc! In 1900, four million records were sold. By 1920, it was 100 million.

That wasn't the end of the music revolution. In the 1920s, new radio technology conquered the world, and it sounded good because high-quality electrical microphones were now being used to capture sound. Radio also changed the sort of music people enjoyed, and Americans fell in love with a type of exciting music made by African-American performers: jazz. A singer called Mamie Smith sold a million copies of her jazz song "Crazy Blues", which, back then, was a mind-blowing number. Actually, it's still impressive now!

MUSIC ON THE MOVE

Gramophone wax discs were replaced by vinyl LP (Long Play) records in 1948. These could fit twenty-one minutes of music on each side. Then in 1963 the Philips company launched the compact cassette tape: a small box with a reel of magnetic tape inside. At first these hissed like an angry snake, but the sound soon improved. Cassette players became cool when they were fitted into cars, and people could sing along to their top tunes while driving. Music had gone mobile!

A huge development came in 1979, with the Sony Walkman, a cassette player with headphones so nobody could judge you for your terrible music taste (confession: I like heavy metal!). A tape could fit maybe twenty songs, and you could listen anywhere, doing anything – running, roller skating, hang-gliding, swimming… OK, maybe not the last one. Next came CDs in 1982, which sounded great, but the best gadget arrived in 1997: the digital MP3 player! This could store hundreds of songs and I remember how thrilling it was to have all my music on one machine! It felt like the future had arrived.

DOG

Do you have an adorable pet to play with this evening? You'd be continuing a very long tradition. Even though animals were often made to do backbreaking work in the past, that didn't mean there weren't also beloved pets. Perhaps the most loved of all was the humble pooch, who has been humankind's slobbering best friend since the Stone Age.

HUMANKIND'S BEST FRIEND

Scientists have spent a lot of time trying to figure out when lovely, cuddly dogs evolved from big, scary wolves. They think it happened at least 15,000 years ago, but some argue it was as far back as 40,000 years ago. One popular theory is that humans deliberately bred tame hunting dogs, by choosing the least aggressive wolf cubs and constantly breeding them together until, after a few generations, the pups were naturally friendly and had evolved to be physically different to wolves. Other scientists say the wolves tamed themselves, by hanging out with humans to enjoy their food and shelters.

Obviously, whatever they did, it worked! But there must have been some slightly scary moments when huge, snarling wolves refused to play fetch, and the Stone Age people suddenly felt like they'd made a bit of a mistake...

Nice wolfie...

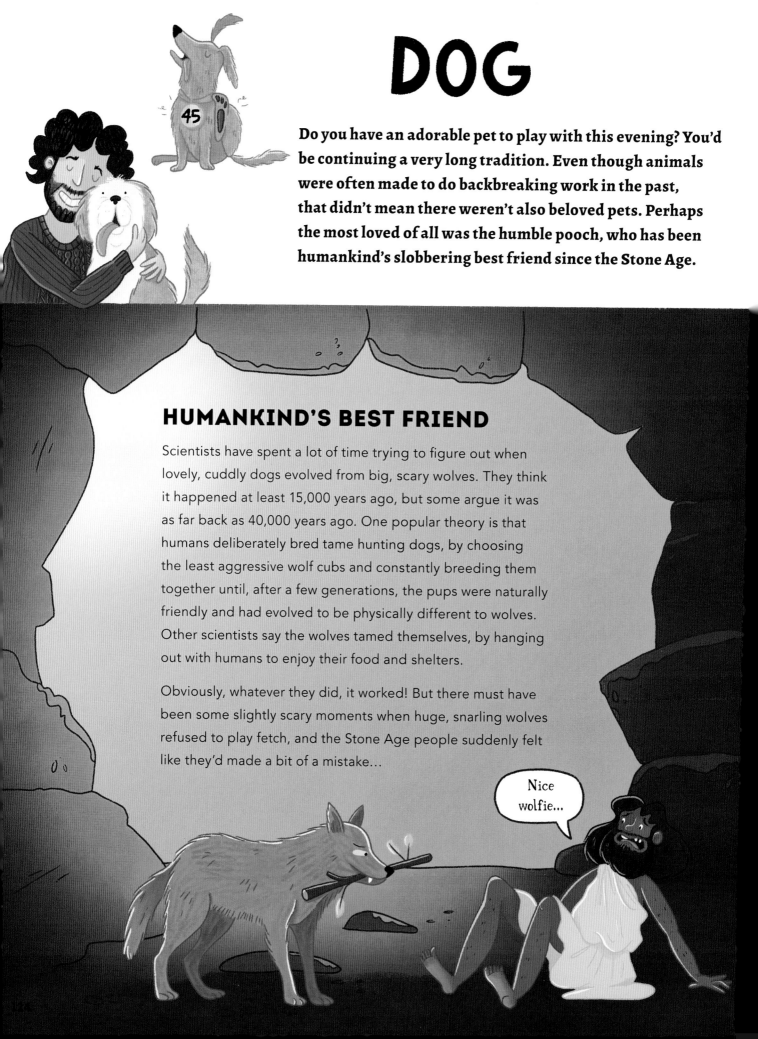

THE HOUNDS OF BABYLON

Once the Stone Age ended, and people started farming and didn't need to hunt for their dinners, they still found a place in their lives for pet pooches. In Bronze Age Mesopotamia (Iraq), about 4,000 years ago, the Babylonians absolutely loved dogs. In their art we see cute dogs going for walkies, or a dog mum nursing a litter of puppies. They also had statues of guard dogs at the entrance to important buildings, protecting the people inside from bad spirits.

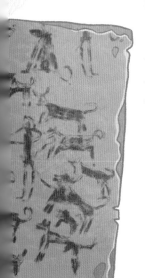

Babylonians associated dogs with Gula, their goddess of healing, who was sometimes shown with a dog next to her feet. If people were mean to a dog, Babylonians believed Gula might not cure their illnesses! We also have evidence that Babylonian kings and posh people hunted for sport, using dogs to help them chase down wild animals.

What I love most about the Babylonians is their many sayings and proverbs about dogs. These were written down in cuneiform (remember that?). These sayings include:

> An old dog which is played with turns into a puppy again.

> In the city with no dogs, the fox is boss.

> A dog said to his master, "If my pleasure is of no importance to you, then my loss should not be either!"

> The blacksmith's dog could not overturn the anvil, so it knocked over the water pot instead.

> The dog understands "Take it!" It does not understand "Put it down!"

These sayings show dogs were treated kindly, and with great affection, but Babylonians also knew dogs could be territorial, stubborn and a bit naughty! It doesn't matter which century you live in, dogs will always want to chew your shoes.

You're definitely a Smylefeste.

WHAT'S IN A NAME?

When our dog scampers off to chase a squirrel, we call its name to bring it back. But what is a good name for a dog? History has some fun answers. Six hundred years ago, the medieval English lord Edward, Duke of York wrote a book called *The Master of Game,* in which he listed over 1,000 names for hunting dogs. Most were descriptions of what the dog did well: Nosewise, Clench and Holdfast were great names for sniffer dogs and strong-jawed biters. Meanwhile, Smylefeste was perhaps for a friendly dog with big, goofy teeth. Oddly, Crab was another common name (that's a totally different animal, isn't it?!), and one of the names he suggested was actually … er … Nameless. Bit weird!

Anne Boleyn, who was King Henry VIII's ill-fated second queen, had a beloved doggy called Purkoy, named after the medieval French word for "why". Apparently, her doggo had a permanently quizzical face, as if she was always asking it to do maths.

The first American president, George Washington, had loads of dogs and gave them very silly names, including Madame Moose, Sweet Lips, Truelove, Tipsy and Drunkard. Those names suggest they weren't very well behaved! One of Washington's naughtiest dogs was called Vulcan, who once ruined a dinner party by stealing an entire roast ham from the table before it could be served. Bad dog, naughty dog!

CAT

Not a dog lover? Then maybe you're a cat person, by which I don't mean an actual human-feline hybrid, because then you'd be a ThunderCat (that would be awesome!). Cats have often had quite a bad reputation in the past, but their story also goes back thousands of years.

TAMING THE TABBY

Unlike dogs, cats definitely seem to have tamed themselves, although all the cats I know love wandering off on their own, so they're clearly still a bit wild. Around 9,500 years ago, in Cyprus, a cat was carefully buried in a grave close to a human, showing it was probably treated as a pet. Chances are it was a wild cat that had originally slunk into the village to hunt the mice and rats that nibbled through the farmers' grain supply.

The farmers would have been delighted to have a professional rodent exterminator in their village. So the cat probably decided to hang around, realising that life was much cushier surrounded by people who might hand over their dinner scraps. That would be no surprise, seeing as most of the cats in my street try to get a second meal by mewling sadly at the back door of their neighbour's house!

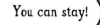

You can stay!

GREG'S GREATEST

UNUSUAL PET

There are many weird pets from history. In the early 1800s, the English poet Lord Byron showed up to university with a pet bear! A few decades later, the French poet Gerard de Nerval walked his pet lobster on a silk leash. And the posh ancient Roman Lucius Licinius Crassus was so fond of his eels, he gave them gold earrings. I didn't even know eels had ears!

47 TV

Though my job as a historian means I spend most of my days reading books, I love to relax on the sofa and watch the box. In this sense, TV is surprisingly ancient, because archaeologists think that sitting together to watch moving images is what Stone Age people did in caves, 20,000 years ago. Amazingly, prehistoric cave art possibly appeared to move when it was illuminated by a flickering fire. However, the TV is a very clever bit of technology, and we can be grateful to one man for its invention.

JOHN LOGIE BAIRD: TV PIONEER

So which genius should we thank for our TVs? John Logie Baird was a brilliant Scottish inventor born in 1888. Even as a teenager he rigged up a telephone system to connect his bedroom to his friends' houses. One day he caused a huge power cut in Glasgow while trying to make artificial diamonds by sending a huge jolt of electricity into a chunk of graphite. Oops!

Baird's next idea was to make inflatable shoes and special quick-drying socks to keep his feet warm. Bit weird, right?! Actually, the socks sold well to soldiers in the muddy trenches of the First World War, which earned Baird enough money to quit his job. Off he went to lovely, sunny Trinidad where he decided to invent … er … a jam factory. Hmm, bit different, but OK! Only later did he move to England and start experimenting with his bold idea of television.

THE FIRST TELEVISIONS

Baird's first design was made in the early 1920s out of biscuit tins, knitting needles, cardboard, a hat box, a pair of scissors, a tea chest and some bicycle lights. Can you imagine inventing a world-famous technology from the random stuff in your cupboard? The BBC allowed Baird to do an experimental broadcast in 1929. Alas, there was only one transmitter tower, so the sound and vision couldn't be broadcast at the same time. Viewers saw the picture for a bit, then heard the sound, then saw the image again. Not ideal! Once that was solved, in 1932 the BBC showed the first TV programme designed to entertain audiences. It had singers, dancers, musicians and even a performing sea lion! However, they all looked ghostly because the picture was black-and-white and made of loads of wobbly lines. Not exactly HD quality...

It wasn't until the 1950s that TV became popular, meaning Baird sadly didn't live long enough to see the huge impact of his work. But what a legacy. Thanks, John!

CHANGE THE CHANNEL

Did you know remote controls are 100 years old? They were originally for changing the radio station. They had to be connected to the radio with a long wire, and it wasn't until 1939 that a wireless one, called the Mystery Control, was invented. And if you think that's a fun name, wait till you hear the next lot!

The first popular TV remote sold in the USA, in 1950, was called the Lazy Bones, because people didn't have to get up to change the channel. You could also buy one called the Blab-Off, which muted the sound during annoying adverts. These remotes were both connected with wires, but then came the Flash-matic, which sent a light signal to the TV. Unfortunately it was unreliable because the light receiver would get confused by sunshine and lamps. Imagine how annoying it would be to miss the ending of your fave TV show because a car drove past with its headlamps on, and your remote control switched the TV off!

48 PYJAMAS

The day is very nearly done, so it's time to clean your teeth and switch your clothes for your comfy PJs (unless you are a professional writer like me, and just wear your pyjamas all day as well!). I suppose the obvious question is why do we wear different clothes to bed? An interesting place to look for answers is the UK in the 1800s.

TO CAP IT ALL OFF

In the 1800s, British men and women wore a nightcap to keep their heads warm while they snoozed. Usually, the chap's cap was long, pointed and a little bit floppy – think of a garden gnome. Ladies, on the other hand, wore a woollen or cotton bonnet that was fitted more closely over the head and held in place by a chin strap. These became very uncool in the early 1900s as they were associated with old grannies, but in the 1920s they became fashionable again when they were renamed *boudoir caps*. These were made of very pretty silk, with tassels, flowers and other needlessly lovely bits dangling off!

Nightcaps kept the heat in, but for ladies they also helped with their beauty regime. A nice bonnet stopped their hair getting all tangled and messy, and it protected elaborate up-do hairstyles so they didn't have to be redone every morning. Ladies also sometimes perfumed their caps, so their hair smelled amazing when they woke up, plus the cap protected the pillow from oily shampoo stains.

Of course, good ideas never go out of fashion, and wearing a silk bonnet is still very popular today, particularly for women of African heritage, whose beautiful, curly hair can be dried out and damaged by rubbing against the pillow.

Did you forget to put your nightcap on again?

NIGHTGOWN IS THE RIGHT GOWN

If you've ever seen a film adaptation of Charles Dickens' famous book *A Christmas Carol* (my fave is the Muppets movie version), you'll remember the grumpy Ebenezer Scrooge being visited by three ghosts while wearing his long nightgown. This was standard night-time clothing in the mid-1800s, particularly in chilly countries like Britain. The nightgown wasn't particularly fancy, it was just a very long, very baggy smock dress, similar to the white thawb robes worn by people in the hot desert countries of the Middle East. Of course, the nightgown was to keep you warm at night, while the thawb was to keep you cool in the daytime – same clothing, opposite purpose!

So toasty!

So cool!

FROM SOLDIERS TO SNOOZERS

Pyjama is an old Persian word, adopted by Hindi and Urdu speakers in South Asia, which means "leg-clothing". PJs are traditionally loose trousers for men and women; the *churidar* style is often tight to the legs, whereas the *salwar* is baggier.

Maybe you wear PJs to bed at night, and they cover your whole body? Well, traditionally pyjamas weren't like that. Indeed, from the late-1700s to the mid-1800s, most of India was run by the British East India Company. This was a mega-powerful business, slightly separate to the British government, that controlled trade, raised taxes and even had its own private armies! These 250,000 soldiers were mostly local Indian recruits who wore a smart, colourful jacket and a pair of white pyjama bottoms. It's not that they'd overslept and raced out of bed without remembering to pull on their proper trousers, these *were* their proper trousers.

So, how come modern PJs cover your top half too? Well, from the 1870s onwards, Brits who'd lived in India started to bring the loose-legged fashion back to the UK. They still wore pyjama bottoms in the daytime, around the house or in the garden, but they also started to wear them during the colder nights, paired with a buttoned-up jacket. By the late 1800s, men's pyjamas often had matching top and bottoms (but it was too early for Spider-Man logos…).

GREG'S GREATEST

PYJAMA HATER

Not everyone was a fan of pyjamas, however. The famous American writer Mark Twain travelled through India in the 1890s, and found it an amazing place, but said, "Pyjamas are hot on a hot night and cold on a cold night – defects which a nightshirt is free from. I tried the pyjamas in order to be in the fashion; but I was obliged to give them up, I couldn't stand them." Twain was very much a nightgown dude.

FASHIONABLE PJS

It wasn't just the fellas who brought pyjamas back from South Asia. Ladies also went in for the matching top and bottoms idea. But whereas chaps only wore them at night, the ladies stuck with daytime too. Famous fashion designers like Coco Chanel helped to make them very *chic* (a French word for elegant and stylish, pronounced "sheek"). These snazzy outfits were often made from slinky silk, satin or rayon (a new artificial fibre invented by scientists), and they were known as beach pyjamas – ideal for relaxing at the seaside – or evening pyjamas, which could be worn while hosting fun dinner parties.

So, if your parents tell you to change out of your PJs before school tomorrow, feel free to tell them that, actually, pyjamas have long been perfectly appropriate daywear … just as long as you haven't spilled your breakfast all over them!

PILLOW 49

Are you a pillow plumper or a pillow squisher? Do you like them fluffy or firm? Well, I'm on Team Squishy. I like a chunky, memory foam pillow that makes a reassuring THWOMP sound when I land on it. Chances are, your pillows are stuffed – maybe with goose down, or feathers, or some other padded material. But in many parts of the world, pillows were traditionally hard. And I mean properly "give-it-a-knock-and-it-goes-donk" hard. A pillow fight with these bad boys would have resulted in a broken nose!

A SOLID NIGHT'S SLEEP

The oldest examples of these solid pillows are from ancient Egypt, over 4,500 years ago. Rather than a fluffy, fabric pillow, Egyptians used wooden headrests that were often thin and U-shaped. They were usually mounted on a beautifully carved stand at the end of the bed. When the snoozer lay down, their head and neck were supported in the centre of the headrest, forcing them to sleep on their back rather than rolling over onto their side.

Why was this preferred, then? These headrests were very common in other places besides Egypt – many African cultures used them, as did Japanese people in the Edo period (which began over 400 years ago) – and they were designed to protect people's braided hairstyles and beautifully oiled wigs from being smooshed into embarrassing morning bedhead. Hair has often been a sign of beauty and power around the world, and people wanted to be able to wake up looking both sensational and respectable, rather than like they'd been dragged backwards through a hedge (which is very much my morning look).

With these headrests, wealthy individuals might have been able to go many days without having to fix their hairstyles – very useful if the hair had been braided, or coated with clay, or had lots of ornaments woven into it (all quite common in Africa's many cultural traditions). Plus, there's just something wonderful about these gorgeously carved headrests; they were beautiful works of art, handcrafted from expensive materials, so they were a great way to show off how important you were.

SLOPING SLUMBERERS

Is your mattress high up off the ground, held up by a bedframe? Mine is! These raised beds date back at least 5,000 years. The preserved Stone Age village of Skara Brae in Orkney (google it!) boasts chunky stone slabs that people slept on thousands of years ago – it's very much like the furniture in the Flintstones cartoon (google it!).

The ancient Egyptians went one better, carving extremely beautiful bedframes with lion's claws for feet. King Tutankhamun was buried with several golden beds just like this, but instead of a headrest it had a footrest. Why? Because Egyptian beds sloped downwards, so a footrest stopped him sliding out and landing on his bum!

FLOOR SNORES

Not every society chose a raised bed. In many parts of Asia and Africa, sleeping has usually been done on the floor. In Western Asia, the medieval Mongols and Turks were famed for living as nomads, meaning they were always moving around and settling only for a short time in different places. They carried everything with them on the backs of their horses and camels. I'm not sure if you've ever tried tying a big wooden bed to a camel, but it's not easy! Much simpler to carry a rolled-up mat, or cushions, which can be packed away with the tent.

Perhaps the most famous floor-snoozers are the Japanese, who often still slumber on long, thin *tatami* mats. They put a thin mattress called a *shikibuton* on top, and then cosy up under a duvet called a *kakebuton*.

No chance.

Please!

PILLOW  49

Are you a pillow plumper or a pillow squisher? Do you like them fluffy or firm? Well, I'm on Team Squishy. I like a chunky, memory foam pillow that makes a reassuring THWOMP sound when I land on it. Chances are, your pillows are stuffed – maybe with goose down, or feathers, or some other padded material. But in many parts of the world, pillows were traditionally hard. And I mean properly "give-it-a-knock-and-it-goes-donk" hard. A pillow fight with these bad boys would have resulted in a broken nose!

A SOLID NIGHT'S SLEEP

The oldest examples of these solid pillows are from ancient Egypt, over 4,500 years ago. Rather than a fluffy, fabric pillow, Egyptians used wooden headrests that were often thin and U-shaped. They were usually mounted on a beautifully carved stand at the end of the bed. When the snoozer lay down, their head and neck were supported in the centre of the headrest, forcing them to sleep on their back rather than rolling over onto their side.

Why was this preferred, then? These headrests were very common in other places besides Egypt – many African cultures used them, as did Japanese people in the Edo period (which began over 400 years ago) – and they were designed to protect people's braided hairstyles and beautifully oiled wigs from being smooshed into embarrassing morning bedhead. Hair has often been a sign of beauty and power around the world, and people wanted to be able to wake up looking both sensational and respectable, rather than like they'd been dragged backwards through a hedge (which is very much my morning look).

With these headrests, wealthy individuals might have been able to go many days without having to fix their hairstyles – very useful if the hair had been braided, or coated with clay, or had lots of ornaments woven into it (all quite common in Africa's many cultural traditions). Plus, there's just something wonderful about these gorgeously carved headrests; they were beautiful works of art, handcrafted from expensive materials, so they were a great way to show off how important you were.

GREG'S GREATEST

Don't worry, I can dream myself better!

DIVINE DREAM DOCTOR

Sleep has often been considered a time of restoration and healing. When ancient Greeks got ill, they'd go to the temple of their healing god, Asclepius, and sleep there overnight. The idea was that a cure would magically come to them in their dreams, and they would wake up knowing how to get better. My dreams are never this useful – I mostly just wake up with achey legs from playing football in my sleep!

PILLOW FILL-OH!

In medieval East Asia, solid headrests were very popular among the rich, and were often painted with lovely artistic scenes. In China, they might be made of porcelain or stoneware, which stayed nice and cool in hot summers. But there was also an even cleverer type of pillow – the hollow one. Chinese and Korean porcelain pillows could be filled with hot water to heat the snoozer's neck in winter, and cool water to avoid a summertime sweat-fest. The Chinese poet Tian Xi, who lived 1,000 years ago, wrote a poem about his "chrysanthemum pillow" (chrysanthemum is a type of flower), which he stuffed with sweet-smelling medicinal herbs to calm his nerves and give him a good night's sleep.

By contrast, an important Chinese historian called Sima Guang, who lived not long after Tian Xi, liked to stay up late and work on his book. To ensure he kept going through the night, he slept on an uncomfortable log that woke him up regularly. He would then get out of bed, rub his sore neck and do some writing until it felt better, before popping back for another power nap. I'm also a historian who likes to stay up late working (I'm writing this at 2 a.m.!), but that sounds like a horrible punishment to me. I'll stick with my memory foam pillow, thanks very much!

BED

Well, it's been a long day of activity, so it's time to settle down for a good snooze so you're refreshed for tomorrow's adventures. I'm guessing your bed looks a lot like mine – a comfy, bouncy mattress with a clean sheet over the top and a nice, soft duvet for maximum snugness. Ooh, toasty! But what did a bed look like thousands of years ago in the Stone Age? Amazingly, archaeologists know the answer.

STONE AGE SNOOZING

Ancient humans often sheltered in caves, and it was at a place called Sibudu Cave, in South Africa, that archaeologists found evidence of prehistoric mattresses dating back 77,000 years. Isn't that incredible?! These mattresses weren't stuffed with springs or fancy memory foam, like ours — no, they were stitched together from leaves and rushes. One of the plants used was river wild quince, which produces a chemical that insects and mosquitos don't like, meaning whoever snoozed on the mattress didn't wake up with itchy bites in the morning. Cunning!

However, we also know that these prehistoric people liked to munch their greasy, meaty dinners in bed. They dropped bits of food and wiped their mucky fingers on the leaves of the mattress, meaning their bedding would eventually attract an army of creepy-crawlies. Yuck! So, how did they deal with that? Scrub it with a brush? Wash it in the river? Nope! They just set the mattress on fire, and then stitched a new one. Definitely DON'T try that at home!

Looks like it's time to set this on fire...

SLOPING SLUMBERERS

Is your mattress high up off the ground, held up by a bedframe? Mine is! These raised beds date back at least 5,000 years. The preserved Stone Age village of Skara Brae in Orkney (google it!) boasts chunky stone slabs that people slept on thousands of years ago – it's very much like the furniture in the Flintstones cartoon (google it!).

The ancient Egyptians went one better, carving extremely beautiful bedframes with lion's claws for feet. King Tutankhamun was buried with several golden beds just like this, but instead of a headrest it had a footrest. Why? Because Egyptian beds sloped downwards, so a footrest stopped him sliding out and landing on his bum!

FLOOR SNORES

Not every society chose a raised bed. In many parts of Asia and Africa, sleeping has usually been done on the floor. In Western Asia, the medieval Mongols and Turks were famed for living as nomads, meaning they were always moving around and settling only for a short time in different places. They carried everything with them on the backs of their horses and camels. I'm not sure if you've ever tried tying a big wooden bed to a camel, but it's not easy! Much simpler to carry a rolled-up mat, or cushions, which can be packed away with the tent.

Perhaps the most famous floor-snoozers are the Japanese, who often still slumber on long, thin *tatami* mats. They put a thin mattress called a *shikibuton* on top, and then cosy up under a duvet called a *kakebuton*.

No chance.

Please!

SLEEP TIGHT

If you've ever had someone tuck you in at night and say "sleep tight", that's a call back to the medieval era! Medieval beds in Europe were straw-filled mattresses plonked onto ropes that stretched across the bedframe. The ropes would gradually stretch and slacken, until the mattress sagged in the middle. So, a good night's sleep required tightening the ropes – hence, sleep tight!

GREG'S GREATEST

GREAT BED OF WARE

How could I not choose a bed with "Great" in its name! This four-poster bed with a canopy (known as a tester) over the top was probably constructed in 1590. It was possibly made as a tourist attraction for an inn in Hertfordshire, England. Why did it attract tourists? Because it's absolutely MASSIVE! At three metres wide, it was made for eight people, but you could probably cram in an entire football team (provided they take off their muddy boots), so even the worst of bed-hoggers would struggle to spreadeagle across it all. We know people wanted to say they'd slept in the bed, because they carved in their initials and left their wax seals on the wood. Even Shakespeare mentions it in his play *Twelfth Night*. This was a very famous bed, but it must have been a right faff to change those huge sheets!

Darling, are you coming to bed?

I'm IN the bed already!

INDEX